ART IN THE KITCHEN

WESTMORELAND
MUSEUM OF ART

Merry Christmas Shirley 1995.

Much love & blessings

Doris Delserone

WOMEN'S COMMITTEE

DEDICATION

*To Dr. Paul A. Chew, gentleman, author, artist, and a generous host and chef, the Women's Committee dedicates this book, **Art in the Kitchen**. During his thirty-five years as director, Dr. Chew not only has brought together an important collection of art works but has created a museum tradition for celebrating art and artist. Enticing the viewer and patron with wonderful and unusual previews and dinners, he has made the museum the center of cultural and social life and the home of delightful gastronomic events creating the perfect accompaniment for the art they celebrated.*

Copyright© 1995 by Westmoreland Museum of Art
221 North Main Street, Greensburg, Pennsylvania 15601, 1-412-837-1500
All Rights Reserved
Library of Congress Number: 95-060117
ISBN: 0-931241-27-8

Edited and Manufactured in the United States of America by:
Favorite Recipes® Press, P.O. Box 305142, Nashville, Tennessee 37230, 1-800-358-0560

First Printing: 1995 7,500 copies

Cover: George Hetzel (1826-1899), *Still Life with Concord Grapes and Apples*, c. 1897.
Oil on Canvas 15¼ x 24½ inches. Gift of William A. Coulter Fund.

Inserts: From the permanent collection of the Westmoreland Museum of Art.
Photography by Richard Stoner.

All recipes in this book have been kitchen tested by members and friends of the
Westmoreland Museum of Art. This cookbook is a collection of our favorite recipes,
which are not necessarily original recipes.

CONTENTS

FOREWORD

When the Cookbook Committee asked me to write this foreword, they suggested I begin with my earliest recollection of interest in food preparation at home. I wouldn't say my mother, Gertrude, or my grandmother, Edith, were bad cooks; they just lacked a pinch of imagination and a dash of curiosity in their kitchen. Family members were delighted when our Aunt Maude, Grandmother's sister, sent over her Irish cook, Phoebe, every Wednesday to bake pies, breads, and cinnamon rolls. Phoebe arrived early Tuesday evening to prepare mounds of dough, which were floured and stored in wooden covered boxes. Returning home from school on Wednesday, I was greeted with the intoxicating aroma of baked goods. When Phoebe noticed my inquisitiveness about baking, she challenged me to prepare her famous banana cake. The finished product to my delight not only surprised me but the entire family. I was thoroughly hooked and went on to baking other recipes and then preparing whole meals for the family.

All of this happened in the middle of the Great Depression while my family lived with my grandmother's family. My mother and grandmother encouraged my interest in cooking, which continued into my college years at the University of Pittsburgh. Virgil Cantini, from whom I rented a studio apartment, was an artistic Italian cook and many of his dishes entered my recipe book. Virgil was an instructor in the Fine Arts Department at the University. Dr. Walter Read Hovey, chairman of the Fine Arts Department, became my good friend, teacher, and mentor. College summers were spent at Walter's home at Chatham, Cape Cod. Rose, his cook, and I planned all the cocktail and dinner parties. Fresh fish was the order of the day and I learned a great deal about fish and fish chowders.

Spending three years at Manchester, England, at the University, won me my Ph.D. degree; I won over my student friends by introducing the American hamburger in all its glory. Art history was my major subject and Continental food became the second course. Student vacations spent in Spain, Holland, and France filled my notebook with artistic revelations as well as gastronomic delights.

When the Board of Trustees elected me the first director of the Westmoreland Museum of Art on December 7, 1957, they also got an eager chef. Food would be used to enhance every exhibition preview, and special dinners celebrated major exhibitions. It just seemed natural to welcome and share fine food and wine with friends, patrons, and guests of the museum, as I would with guests at my home. Our gatherings celebrated both the art that surrounded us and the event.

One exhibition in particular comes to mind as a gastronomic event— **Art and the Kitchen**, held in the spring of 1975. The exhibition included paintings, sculptures, and prints of the genre of food as well as the decorative arts found in the kitchen and dining room. Three dinners, each a week apart, were held to celebrate the exhibition. The American menu featured New England Clam Bisque and a Roast Fillet of Texas Beef; the Italian dinner served Minestrone and Saltimbocca; and the French dinner began with Onion Soup Gratinée followed by Roast Chicken a la Normande.

I was very pleased that the Women's Committee used a variation of the title of this exhibition for their cookbook, **Art in the Kitchen**. I have enjoyed working with this dedicated committee, especially enjoying the many abundant and caloric "food tasting" meetings at which aromas and tastes abounded in the museum's kitchen!

Buon appetito!

Paul A. Chew

Paul A. Chew, Director Emeritus

PREFACE

It is with great pride that the Women's Committee of the Westmoreland Museum of Art presents to you our museum and our cookbook.

The museum opened in 1959 and maintains an outstanding collection of works. Representation from the 18th century to the present by nationally recognized American artists includes an emphasis on the art of Pennsylvania with a special interest in the paintings of the southwestern region. From its first acquisition of Rembrandt Peale's *Port-hole Portrait of George Washington*, the collection has grown to over 3,400 works. An additional 2,000 objects comprise an extraordinary antique toy and train collection. As a regional and community resource, the museum, with its varied programs, continues to attract and inspire a growing audience.

Art in the Kitchen is a sampling of recipes collected from this audience. It reflects the diverse tastes and styles of artists, collectors, patrons, friends, relatives, members of the Women's Committee, and staff. We trust our cookbook is one that everyone will enjoy reading and using. We offer additional guidance with some recipes as to preparation and presentation, but ultimately, the art in the kitchen is *your* style, your creativity. In *your* kitchen, *you* are the artist.

THE ART OF THE MENU

Let the dishes be few in number, but exquisitely choice and the wines of the first quality, each in its design;

Let the service of the former proceed from the most sublime to the lightest, and of the latter, from the mildest to the most perfumed.

Let the progress of the events be slow, for dinner is the last business of the day, and let the guests comfort themselves like travelers drawing near their journeys end together. —***The Pleasures of the Table***—Brillat Savarin (1755–1826)

A perfect meal is a work of art, and like a work of art it can be many things. The meal can be simple and satisfying—a bowl of nourishing soup, a salad, a crusty French bread, a piece of cheese, and a fine bottle of wine. The meal can also be complex and elegant—a cup of clear soup, a fish course, entrée, (accompanied by appropriate wines), followed by a salad of mixed greens, cheese, and a refreshing dessert. When designing the menu, plan as if you were painting the meal. Visualize the parts that will make up the whole presentation, selecting foods and garnishes that complement or contrast provocatively, yet pleasingly—the ways colors and techniques work together in a fine painting.

In devising the perfect meal consider several factors: the occasion, number of guests, time of year, hour of day, and preparation time available. Consider also your necessary serving utensils and platters. The menu should be a psychological continuum of sensuous sights, textures, odors, and temperatures. Keep the palate fresh, surprised, and excited throughout the meal. Combine interesting, contrasting colors. Serve foods with different textures. Juxtapose cold and hot, crisp and creamy, rough and smooth, sauced and dry. Imagine how foods will look and taste together.

A well-planned meal teases the imagination, offers constant surprise and pleasure, yet has a specific plan. Courses should be designed to heighten the appetite. Hors d'oeuvres and appetizers must be light in body, never sweet nor overabundant. Each course should provide a happy contrast to the one preceding and the one following. At the same time, the progression of tastes should move from light, delicate, and complex to those which are robust, rich, and simple. Wine should be chosen similarly. Once introduced to a pungent taste, the palate cannot return to a bland one with any joy. Decide whether

a dish will "kill" anything that follows due to its spice or garlic content. If so, this dish should probably be the climax of the meal. Avoid excessive repetition of ingredients and cooking methods. For instance, one creamed dish is sufficient...as is one cooked with wine.

There are dishes known to kill accompanying wines and vice versa. Wines often overpower eggs. The acidity of a vinaigrette can spoil a wine. Sweetness tends to satisfy the palate and should be saved for the finale. It is wise to think of dishes in terms of their impact on the senses:

> Is a dish hot / lukewarm / cold?
> Is the texture smooth / rough / crunchy?
> Is it frivolous / serious in intent?
> Is it delicate / moderate / robust in flavor?
> Is it elegant / peasant in presentation?
> Is it colorful / neutral in appearance?
> Is it sauced / unsauced? Dry / juicy?

By considering these characteristics you can "sketch" your own preliminary menu. Keeping in mind the preferences of your guests, select your entrée first and plan the remaining courses accordingly. For example:

> **First course**—warm, peasant, moderate flavor, juicy
> **Second course**—hot, elegant, neutral, smooth, serious
> **Third course**—hot, colorful, robust
> **Salad**—frivolous, cold, peasant
> **Dessert**—neutral, crunchy, dry

Finally in organizing a menu consider its presentation—it is nearly as important to flatter the eye as it is the palate. Don't serve spinach on a green plate or a tomato sauce on a red one. Don't sprinkle handfuls of chopped parsley over everything. If possible, garnish a dish with an ingredient in its composition. Combine interesting contrasting colors in foods and on serving pieces. Let the pleasures of your table be found in the artful preparation and presentation of your menu.

Linda Austin, member IACP
International Association of Culinary Professionals

THE FOUNDER'S LEGACY

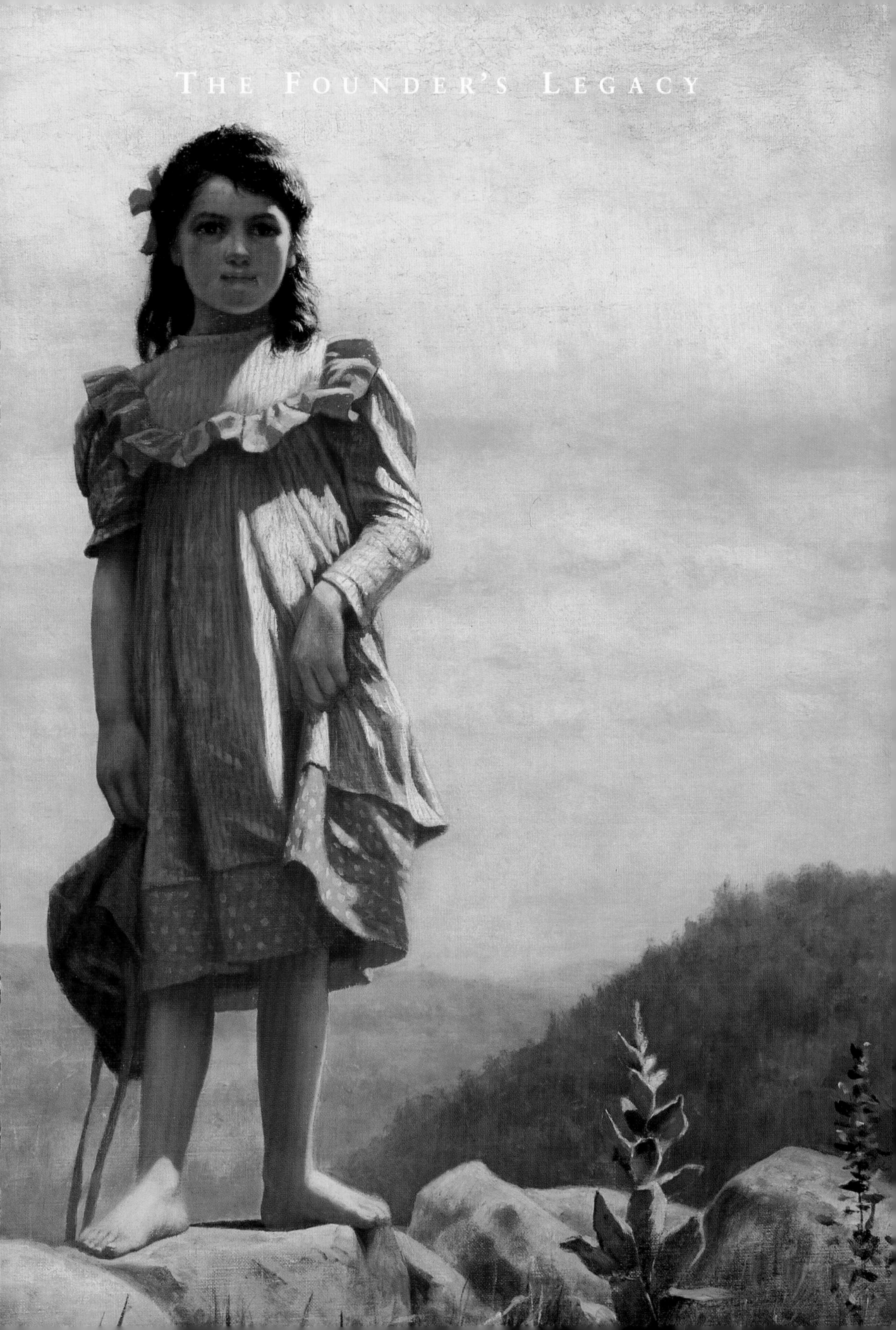

THE FOUNDER'S LEGACY

In the hands of an uncommon woman, a tradition makes reality of dreams. The dream was to create a museum; the tradition, public service; the woman, Mary Marchand Woods. The Westmoreland Museum of Art is the benefaction of Mrs. Cyrus E. Woods to the community of her birth and home of her ancestors. Following the tradition of six generations of Marchand women, she married into public service. Mr. Woods, a native of Clearfield County, served in state government before being appointed Minister to Portugal in 1912, Ambassador to Spain, 1921–23, and Ambassador to Japan, 1923–24. After his death, Mrs. Woods created the Woods-Marchand Foundation for the future erection and support of a museum she had long envisioned as a center for pictorial and decorative arts. Erected on the site of her home, the museum opened in 1959, six years after her death.

Mrs. Woods was a collector of Americana, European, and Oriental objects. Preserved among the effects of her estate were her childhood toys and her mother's manuscript cookbook. Mrs. Marchand's scrapbook, *Recipes—my Friends' and my own!* (1906), recalls memories of a household where entertaining was enjoyed and cooking was a pleasure. Its charm suggested the theme for this section of recipes that have similarly passed from mother to daughter, from friend to friend, and from our Museum to its guests.

John George Brown, N.A. (1831-1913)
Maid of the Hills
Oil on Canvas, 30 x 25 inches
Gift of Elizabeth Braun Ernst

DELLA ROBBIA BRIE

36 servings

This was the fruit and cheese course for the McKenna gourmet dinner that was held November 8, 1980. Wine served as a complement was Chateau Leoville Barton, St. Julien 1973. A beautiful, edible interpretation of a Della Robbia wreath.

Frosted Grape Clusters
1 large Red Delicious
    apple
1 large Golden Delicious
    apple
1 large Granny Smith
    apple
1 large Bosc pear
1 large Anjou pear
2 teaspoons Fruit-Fresh
3 tablespoons water

1 (2-pound) wheel of
    Brie cheese
1 (12-ounce) package
    dried figs
1 (8-ounce) package
    dates
1 (6-ounce) package
    dried apricots
12 large strawberries

Prepare Grape Clusters.

Core and slice the apples and pears lengthwise. Mix Fruit Fresh with the water. Dip the slices in mixture; drain.

Place the cheese on a round cheese board in the center of a large serving platter. Alternate small groupings of apples, grapes, pears, figs and dates around the cheese, leaving a small amount of space between the fruit and cheese.

Position the apricots and strawberries in a circle between the cheese and the arranged fruit.

FROSTED GRAPE CLUSTERS

5 grape clusters

5 small clusters of
    seedless black, green
    and/or red grapes
2 egg whites, slightly
    beaten
½ cup superfine sugar

Dip the grape clusters into the egg whites and sprinkle with the sugar to coat. Chill the grapes for 15 to 20 minutes; repeat the process.
—*Joan Beidler*

PÂTÉ EMERITUS

36 servings

6 spinach leaves
3 (4-ounce) slices ham

1/2 cup minced onion
2 tablespoons butter
1/2 cup Cognac

1 pound beef liver
2 eggs, lightly beaten
1 pound lean ground beef
1/4 teaspoon pepper
1 1/2 teaspoons salt
1 teaspoon allspice
1/2 teaspoon thyme
2 cloves of garlic,
   pressed

8 slices bacon
2 bay leaves

Preheat the oven to 350 degrees.

Blanch the spinach leaves in boiling water in a saucepan for 1 minute; drain. Cut each ham slice lengthwise into halves. Wrap the ham strips with the spinach leaves; set aside.

Sauté the onion in the butter in a skillet over low heat until translucent. Remove the onion to a medium bowl. Add the Cognac to the skillet. Cook until reduced by half and add to the onion.

Cut the liver into 1/4-inch cubes. Combine the liver with the eggs, ground beef, onion mixture, pepper, salt, allspice, thyme and garlic in a bowl; mix well with hands or a wooden spoon.

Grease an 8-cup loaf pan or rectangular or oval terrine. Press 1/3 of the liver mixture evenly in the pan; add a layer of 3 spinach-wrapped ham slices. Repeat the layers, ending with the liver mixture. Pat firmly with a wooden spoon.

Poach the bacon strips in a small pan of boiling water for 6 minutes; drain well. Arrange on top of the layers and press flat. Place the bay leaves on the bacon.

Cover the pan tightly with foil and place the lid on top. Place the loaf pan in a large baking pan. Add boiling water to half fill the baking pan.

Bake at 350 degrees for 1 1/2 hours.

Weight the pâté by placing a 3- or 4-pound weight on top of the foil. Place a board on the foil before adding the weights if necessary.

Let the pâté cool to room temperature. Chill, weighted, in the refrigerator. Unmold the pâté onto a serving platter. —*Dr. Paul A. Chew*

A traditional garnish for a pâté would be small gherkins or cubes of aspic made from the juices of the cooked pâté.

MAY WINE PUNCH

90 servings

Sweet woodruff is an attractive ground cover that broadcasts its aroma each May. It is traditionally used to flavor May wine for May Day celebrations.

2 tablespoons dried
   sweet woodruff
10 bottles Reisling wine
1 bottle Champagne,
   chilled
2 ounces Benedictine
2 ounces brandy

1/2 cup superfine sugar
1 quart sparkling water
1 quart hulled
   strawberries

Steep the sweet woodruff in 1 bottle of the Reisling wine for 6 hours. Combine in a punch bowl with the remaining wine, Champagne, liqueur and brandy; stir well.

Dissolve the sugar in the sparkling water. Add the sugar mixture to the wine punch; mix well. Spoon the strawberries into the punch. Chill the punch by placing a pitcher of crushed ice in the center of the punch bowl.

Ladle into punch cups to serve. —*Lucia Coulter*

WOMEN'S COMMITTEE CHICKEN SALAD

10 servings

Serve this hot chicken salad with a fruit salad and Zucchini-Basil Muffins for a delicious lunch (see page 74).

4 cups diced cooked
   chicken breasts
1 cup mayonnaise
1 cup sour cream
1/4 cup lemon juice
4 cups thinly sliced
   celery
1 1/2 teaspoons dried
   minced onion
1 cup slivered almonds

2 cups seasoned croutons
1 cup shredded Cheddar
   cheese

Preheat the oven to 450 degrees.

Combine the chicken, mayonnaise, sour cream, lemon juice, celery, onion and almonds in a bowl; mix well. Spoon the mixture into an ungreased 9x13-inch baking dish.

Process the croutons in a food processor. Combine the croutons and the cheese; stir well. Sprinkle on top of the chicken mixture. Bake at 450 degrees for 15 to 20 minutes or until bubbly.

CHICKEN SALAD SANDWICH LOAF

14 servings

During the early years of the Women's Committee, which began in 1960, this was often served at special functions. It makes a wonderful, old-fashioned no-frills chicken salad which could easily stand alone.

4 tablespoons vegetable oil
2 tablespoons white wine vinegar
Salt to taste
2 teaspoons seasoned salt
6 cups finely chopped cooked chicken

Homemade Mayonnaise (see below)
2 cups finely chopped celery

1 loaf unsliced white bread
1 loaf unsliced whole wheat bread
16 ounces cream cheese, softened

Combine the oil, vinegar, salt and seasoned salt in a bowl. Add the chicken; mix well. Chill, covered for 8 to 10 hours. Reserve 4 teaspoons of the Homemade Mayonnaise. Add the celery and remaining mayonnaise to the chicken; mix well.

Remove the crust from each bread loaf and slice each loaf horizontally into 4 portions. Reshape into loaves by spreading chicken salad between alternating layers of white and wheat bread. Press to make firm.

Beat the cream cheese in a mixer bowl. Add the reserved mayonnaise; mix well. Spread the cream cheese mixture over each loaf, spreading to cover the sides well.

Chill until serving time for easier slicing.

HOMEMADE MAYONNAISE

2 cups

2 egg yolks
2 tablespoons vinegar
1 teaspoon salt
3/4 cup olive oil
3/4 cup salad oil

Combine the egg yolks, vinegar and salt in a mixer bowl; beat well. Add the olive oil and salad oil; blend gradually until smooth. Chill, covered.

May add lemon juice to thin the mixture.
—*Sarah Collins*

Decorate the sandwich loaf with paprika, parsley and sliced stuffed olives arranged in flower designs.

DR. CHEW'S CREAMY PEA SOUP

8 servings

This lovely bright green soup is served often at Women's Committee luncheons. May be served hot or cold, omitting cream if serving hot.

3/4 cup chopped onion
2 tablespoons butter
1 (46-ounce) can
    chicken broth
8 large spinach leaves,
    stems removed
1/4 teaspoon savory
1/4 teaspoon marjoram
1/4 teaspoon white pepper
2 (16-ounce) packages
    frozen peas
1/2 cup light cream

Soften the onions in butter in a stockpot over low heat. Add the chicken stock. Bring to a boil; reduce heat. Simmer for 7 minutes.

Add the spinach leaves, savory, marjoram and white pepper; mix well. Simmer for 5 minutes. Add the peas; simmer, uncovered, for 4 or 5 minutes or until tender-crisp; the peas should retain their bright green color.

Purée the mixture 1/2 at a time in a blender or food processor.

Pour into a soup tureen. Add the cream before serving. Garnish with a dash of cumin or other fresh herbs. —*Dr. Paul A. Chew*

BASIL CHERRY TOMATOES

10 servings

This is an easy and colorful dish to add to almost any menu.

3 tablespoons butter or
    olive oil
2 tablespoons chopped
    fresh basil
6 cups cherry tomatoes
1 teaspoon lemon juice
Salt and pepper to taste

Melt the butter in a large skillet over medium heat. Add the basil; cook for 2 minutes, stirring constantly. Add the tomatoes; cook for about 3 minutes. Add the lemon juice, salt and pepper; mix well.

Continue stirring until the tomatoes begin to burst. Remove from the heat; serve immediately.

Substitute 1 tablespoon dried basil for the 2 tablespoons chopped fresh basil if desired.
—*Win Beidler*

THE PLAIN BASIC OMELET

1 serving

Rudy Standish, a guest chef at the museum, is renowned from New York City to Washington, D.C., to Dallas, Texas for his omelets.

3 eggs
1 tablespoon cold water
Tabasco sauce to taste
1/4 teaspoon salt
1 tablespoon lightly
   salted butter

Beat the eggs and water with a wire whisk until they look "stringy" and make threads when you lift up the whisk

Heat a skillet over medium heat until several drops of water flicked into the pan "dance" on the hot surface. Add the butter. Hold the skillet in the left hand. Pour the eggs into the skillet; stir with the flat side of a fork in a fast circular motion, shaking the skillet in a rocking motion to keep the eggs from sticking. Spread the eggs evenly to cover any breaks and allow the eggs to set.

Tilt the skillet and fold the outer edge of the omelet over; slide onto a warm plate.

OMELET PARTY FOR TWELVE

12 servings

24 eggs
1/4 cup cold water
1/2 teaspoon Tabasco
   sauce
1 teaspoon salt
12 tablespoons lightly
   salted butter

1/2 cup mixed finely
   chopped fresh
   parsley, chives,
   tarragon or basil
1 pound bacon,
   crisp-cooked,
   crumbled
2 cups shredded Swiss
   or Cheddar cheese or
   grated Parmesan
   cheese
1 pound mushrooms,
   chopped, sautéed

Prepare the egg mixture as above. Use 1 table-spoon butter and 1/2 cup of the egg mixture for each omelet and cook the omelets 1 at a time as above.

Allow each guest to finish his own omelet by choosing what he likes best from the suggested garnishes. —*Rudy Standish,* "**The Omelet King**"

To create an omelet party for twelve, first assemble the ingredients. Then, provide a generous array of garnishes and dazzle your guests with to-order omelets in just 1 minute each.

THE PARTY HAM

20 servings

This party ham is a favorite at museum parties and summer receptions.

1 (10-pound) ham
2 tablespoons cloves
1 (12-ounce) can beer

1/2 cup Dijon mustard
2 cups packed brown
   sugar
1/2 teaspoon marjoram

Preheat the oven to 350 degrees.

Cut diagonal slices 1/4 to 1 1/2-inches apart through the skin and fat on one side of the ham. Reverse the cutting to make diamond shapes. Insert a clove in the middle of each diamond. Pour the beer over the ham.

Place on a rack in a baking pan. Bake at 350 degrees for 20 minutes or until the slices open showing the meat.

Mix the mustard, brown sugar and marjoram in a bowl. Spread the mixture over the ham and into the slices.

Reduce the oven temperature to 225 degrees. Bake for 2 hours, basting every 20 minutes. Serve on a platter with a border of parsley.
—*Dr. Paul A. Chew*

HAM SLICE WITH POTATOES

4 servings

This is a very easy and tasty dish for supper served with savory green beans and a mandarin orange salad. Recipe taken from Mrs. Marchand's scrapbook, "Recipes, my Friends', and my own!" (1906).

1 (1 1/4-pound) ham slice
1 1/2 cups sliced new red
   potatoes, 1/2-inch thick
1 cup (about) milk
1 tablespoon butter
Salt and pepper to taste

Preheat the oven to 350 degrees.

Place the ham slice in a baking pan and layer with the potatoes. Add enough milk to cover. Dot with butter. Sprinkle with salt and pepper to taste.

Bake, covered, at 350 degrees for 1 hour.

Garnish with chopped parsley and serve immediately. —*Elizabeth T. Eccles Jamison*

ROAST RACK OF LAMB

8 servings

This entrée was served November 8,1980 to Mr. and Mrs. J. Cleveland McKenna and guests in the English room, the larger paneled room in the Museum Annex. Those attending were the winners of the Women's Committee fund raising raffle; the prize was awarded at the Museum Ball.

3 racks of lamb, enough for one (16-rib) crown roast

1 cup finely chopped onion

²/₃ cup finely chopped celery

1 bunch finely chopped fresh parsley

1 bunch finely chopped fresh mint

Salt and pepper to taste

Dry white wine to taste

Preheat the oven to 450 degrees.

French cut the bone ends, removing all meat and fat. Shape the ribs into a crown and tie or sew together—or ask your friendly butcher to do this for you. Place crown roast into an oiled roasting pan.

Combine the onion, celery, parsley and mint in a bowl; mix well. Fill the center of the crown with the mixture. Sprinkle the lamb with salt and pepper. Cover the rib ends with foil to prevent burning.

Roast at 450 degrees for 10 minutes. Reduce the oven temperature to 325 degrees. Add dry white wine to the pan. Roast the lamb for 1½ hours or until done to taste, basting frequently with the wine and pan drippings. Remove to a serving platter.

Cover the rib ends with paper frills or mushroom caps and serve 2 ribs per person. —*Joan Beidler*

GARLIC-MUSTARD GLAZE FOR LAMB

Try this alternate taste sensation and serve with Wild Rice and Apricot Stuffing (see page 135) which may be baked separately and spooned into the crown of the lamb just before serving.

¼ cup Dijon mustard

2 tablespoons vegetable oil

2 medium cloves of garlic, crushed

1 teaspoon dried rosemary, crumbled

¼ teaspoon freshly ground pepper

Combine the mustard, oil, garlic, rosemary and pepper in a bowl; mix well. Brush on the lamb before roasting.

LUCIA'S LAMB STEW

8 servings

Make this easy to prepare delicious stew a day ahead for the best flavor. It also freezes well for future meals.

1/4 cup butter
1 medium onion, thinly
    sliced
1 teaspoon paprika
2 pounds lamb shoulder
    or leg, cut into 1-inch
    pieces
1 cup tomato purée
1 cup beef stock
Bouquet garni
1 clove
1 cup sliced mushrooms
5 medium potatoes,
    quartered

3/4 cup cooked green peas
1 cup sour cream
Chopped parsley to taste

Melt the butter in a skillet; add the onion. Sauté the onion until light golden brown. Sprinkle with paprika. Add the lamb pieces; cook until light brown.

Place the onion and lamb in a stew pot. Add the tomato purée, stock, bouquet garni, clove, mushrooms and potatoes; mix well.

Bring to a boil; reduce heat. Simmer, covered, for 1 hour or until the potatoes are tender.

Remove the bouquet garni and clove. Add the peas and sour cream. Heat to serving temperature but do not allow the stew to boil.

Sprinkle with parsley just before serving.
—Lucia Coulter

To make your own bouquet garni, try the following recipe:
1 bay leaf, 1 tablespoon dried tarragon, 1 tablespoon dried parsley, 1 teaspoon dried rosemary, 1 teaspoon dried thyme and 6 peppercorns. Place in a cheesecloth pouch. Store in an airtight container. Use to flavor soups, stews or sauces. Any combination of dried herbs can be used.

BANANA CAKE

12 servings

Add a touch of banana to your day with this cake, which is often served at committee meetings. If you like a more moist cake, use the higher amount of buttermilk suggested. For a festive presentation, spread the baked layers with whipped cream and top with sliced bananas or fresh strawberries. Brush the banana slices with a little fresh lemon juice to help prevent darkening.

2¼ cups sifted cake flour
2½ teaspoons baking
  powder
½ teaspoon baking soda
½ teaspoon salt

½ cup shortening
1¼ cups sugar
2 eggs
1 teaspoon vanilla
1 cup mashed ripe
  bananas
¼ to ½ cup buttermilk

Preheat the oven to 375 degrees.

Sift the flour, baking powder, baking soda and salt together 3 times and set aside.

Combine the shortening and sugar in a mixer bowl; beat until light and fluffy. Add the eggs 1 at a time, beating well after each addition. Add the vanilla to the sugar mixture.

Combine the bananas and the buttermilk in a bowl; mix well. Add the dry ingredients and the banana mixture to the sugar mixture alternately, beating well after each addition. Pour into 2 greased and floured 8½-inch cake pans.

Bake at 375 degrees for 30 minutes. Cool in the pans for about 15 minutes; remove to a wire rack to cool completely.

Spread your favorite vanilla frosting between layers and over the top and sides of the cake.

This cake also works well in a bundt pan.
—Dr. Paul A. Chew

POOR MAN'S CAKES 1892

15 servings

A Pierce family recipe brought from England, the cake got its name at a time when eggs and butter were a luxury that only the rich could afford. The cake requires neither and can be made ahead of time. Serve it plain with a cup of coffee or with vanilla ice cream. It will keep for weeks and will improve in flavor.

1 (15-ounce) package
  raisins
2 cups cold water

2 cups sugar
1/2 cup shortening
1 cup cold water
4 cups flour
1 tablespoon baking soda
1 teaspoon cinnamon
1 teaspoon ground cloves
1 teaspoon nutmeg

Preheat the oven to 350 degrees.

Combine the raisins and 2 cups water in a saucepan. Bring to a boil and simmer for 10 minutes.

Cream the sugar and shortening in a bowl until light and fluffy. Add the undrained raisins and 1 cup cold water; mix well.

Combine the flour, baking soda, cinnamon, cloves and nutmeg in a bowl. Add the flour mixture to the creamed mixture; mix well. Place into 2 greased and floured loaf pans.

Bake at 350 degrees for 45 to 60 minutes or until the loaves test done. Remove the loaves to a wire rack to cool. Keep the loaves tightly wrapped and slice as desired.

May add 1 cup chopped walnuts to the batter if desired. —*Barbara Pierce*

COCOA BAVARIAN NOTE

8 servings

This noteworthy delight was a smashing success served at the 1992 Museum Ball "Artistic Notes." The Bavarian was cut into a musical note for each serving and placed on a musical staff design made by piping chocolate onto the Crème Anglaise.

3 envelopes unflavored
   gelatin
1½ cups cold milk
1¼ cups sugar
¾ cup baking cocoa
1 tablespoon light corn
   syrup
3 tablespoons butter
1¾ cups milk
2 tablespoons vanilla
   extract
1 cup whipping cream,
   whipped
Crème Anglaise
   (see below)

Sprinkle the gelatin over 1½ cups cold milk in a medium saucepan; soften for 3 to 4 minutes. Combine the sugar and baking cocoa in a bowl. Add to the gelatin mixture with the corn syrup.

Bring to a boil over medium heat, stirring constantly. Remove from heat; add the butter. Blend in the 1¾ cups milk and vanilla; mix well. Chill for 2 hours or until almost set.

Beat the chilled mixture until smooth. Fold in the whipped cream. Pour into a 10x15-inch baking pan lined with plastic wrap. Chill until set. Unmold and cut into desired shapes with a cookie cutter. Place on a glass serving plate napped with a thin layer of Crème Anglaise. A design may be piped on top of the custard to complement the shape of the cutouts.

CRÈME ANGLAISE

2¼ cups

1¾ cups half-and-half
1 whole vanilla bean,
   split lengthwise
2 eggs
¼ cup sugar

Place the half-and-half and vanilla bean in a saucepan; bring just to a boil. Remove the saucepan from heat. Scrape the seeds from the vanilla bean into the saucepan, reserving the pod for another use.

Combine the eggs and sugar in a bowl; whisk until fluffy. Add the hot half-and-half in a stream, beating constantly. Place the custard in a saucepan.

Cook over low heat until thickened or to 170 degrees on a candy thermometer, stirring constantly; do not boil. Strain through a fine sieve into a metal bowl. Set the bowl into a larger bowl of ice and cold water. Chill, covered, for 2 hours or for up to 2 days. —*Greensburg Country Club*

CHOCOLATE CHARLOTTE

18 servings

An elegant dessert, this recipe was provided by the first president of the Womens' Committee, Mrs. John B. Steel. The chocolate filling may also be served in white ramekins as a chocolate mousse.

8 (1-ounce) squares
    sweet German's
    chocolate
1½ tablespoons water
4 egg yolks
2 tablespoons sugar
4 egg whites
1 cup whipping cream
2 teaspoons vanilla
    extract
18 ladyfingers, split

1 cup whipping cream
1 teaspoon vanilla extract
1 tablespoon
    confectioners' sugar
4 cups fresh raspberries

Line an 8-cup charlotte mold with waxed paper, leaving several inches of the waxed paper extending over the edge to facilitate removing the charlotte from the mold. Line the bottom and sides of the waxed paper-lined mold with ladyfingers, slightly overlapping the ladyfingers on the sides.

Melt the chocolate with 1½ tablespoons water in a double boiler over hot water, stirring frequently. Remove from heat and allow to cool briefly.

Add the egg yolks 1 at a time, beating well after each addition. Stir in the sugar.

Beat the egg whites in a bowl until stiff peaks form. Mix a small amount of the beaten egg whites into the chocolate mixture. Fold in the remaining egg whites.

Whip 1 cup of the cream in a bowl with 2 teaspoons of the vanilla until almost stiff. Fold into the chocolate mixture.

Spoon the chocolate mixture into the prepared mold. Chill for 12 hours.

Unmold the charlotte onto a serving plate; remove the waxed paper.

Beat the remaining 1 cup whipping cream with the remaining teaspoon vanilla and confectioners' sugar. Arrange the raspberries around the charlotte on the plate. Top the charlotte with a crown of whipped cream rosettes. May serve additional raspberries and whipped cream with the charlotte if desired. —*Madge Steel*

For a beautiful presentation, serve the charlotte on a large, round white platter, dotted with fresh raspberries.

FROZEN PUDDING

8 servings

This refreshing dessert from Mrs. Marchand's scrapbook, "Recipes, my Friends', and my own!" (1906), can be made several days in advance of serving.

1 cup milk
¼ cup flour
1 cup sugar
1 egg, slightly beaten
1 package unflavored
  gelatin
¼ cup cold water
3 tablespoons sherry
2 cups whipping cream
Montrose Sauce or
  Melba Sauce
  (see page 25)

Scald the milk in a saucepan over low heat.

Combine the flour and sugar in a double boiler over hot water.

Stir the scalded milk into the flour mixture gradually. Cook for 7 to 10 minutes or until the mixture thickens slightly.

Stir 1 tablespoon of the hot mixture into the beaten egg. Stir the egg mixture into the hot mixture. Cook for 2 minutes longer, stirring constantly.

Soften the gelatin in the cold water in a saucepan. Bring to a boil over low heat, stirring constantly until the gelatin dissolves.

Add the gelatin to the milk mixture just before removing from heat; blend well. Let stand until cool.

Blend the sherry and whipping cream gradually into the milk mixture. Pour into a shallow freezer container and freeze for 8 to 10 hours.

Cut into individual servings. Place the frozen pudding on dessert plates. Let stand until slightly softened.

Top with the Montrose Sauce or Melba Sauce on the following page.

The Montrose Sauce is off-white and the dessert should be served on a glass or colorful plate with a fruit or holly garnish. The Melba Sauce is a raspberry red. Serve on a glass or dark plate with fresh raspberries if possible.

MONTROSE SAUCE

1 1/2 cups

1 cup light cream
1 egg yolk, beaten
1 tablespoon
   confectioners' sugar
1/2 teaspoon vanilla
1 tablespoon brandy
2 tablespoons sherry

Heat the light cream in a double boiler over hot water over low heat, stirring frequently.

Combine the egg yolk and the confectioners' sugar in a bowl and mix well. Stir a small amount of hot cream into the egg yolk mixture; stir the egg into the hot cream.

Cook until the mixture thickens enough to coat a wooden spoon, stirring constantly.

Remove from heat. Add the vanilla, brandy and sherry; blend well.

Chill for 2 hours before serving.

MELBA SAUCE

1 1/2 cups

1 (10-ounce) package
   frozen raspberries
Sugar to taste

Purée the frozen raspberries in a food processor or blender.

Press the puréed raspberries through a fine sieve to remove the seeds.

Add sugar to taste and mix well.

Chill until serving time. —*Mary Todd Marchand*

The duty of a good cuisinier is to transmit to the generations who will replace him everything he has learned and experienced.
—Fernand Point (1897–1955), Restaurateur

ROYAL LEMON CUSTARD MERINGUE

8 servings

This rich custard dessert was prepared by Betty Hammer at a gourmet dinner at the Museum in April, 1982.

4 eggs whites, at room temperature
1/4 teaspoon cream of tartar or 1 teaspoon white vinegar
1 cup superfine sugar

4 egg yolks, beaten
1/2 cup superfine sugar
1/4 cup fresh lemon juice
1 tablespoon grated lemon rind

1 cup whipping cream, whipped
1 1/2 tablespoons grated lemon rind

Preheat the oven to 250 degrees.

Beat the egg whites until frothy. Add the cream of tartar, beating until stiff peaks form.

Add the 1 cup sugar gradually, beating until stiff peaks form.

Spread the meringue 1/2 to 3/4 inch thick on a buttered pie plate, shaping the sides of the meringue higher than the center.

Bake at 250 degrees for 1 1/4 hours. Reduce the oven temperature to 200 degrees. Bake for 1 hour longer or until meringue is firm and dry. Let stand in closed oven until cool.

Combine the egg yolks, 1/2 cup sugar, lemon juice and 1 tablespoon lemon rind in a double boiler over hot water; blend well.

Cook until thick, beating constantly. Let stand until cool.

Fold 1/2 cup of the whipped cream and 4 teaspoons of the lemon rind gently into the Lemon Custard. Spread half the remaining whipped cream on the meringue. Layer custard and remaining whipped cream on top. Sprinkle with the remaining 1/2 teaspoon lemon rind. Chill for 8 hours.

Garnish with lemon slices and mint sprigs.
—*Betty Hammer*

PREVIEWS

A portion of the Permanent Collection is always on display at the Museum. In addition, changing exhibitions of American art are featured each year. Some noteworthy past and upcoming exhibitions include: "George Hetzel and the Scalp Level Tradition; George Luks — Expressionist Master of Color: Watercolors Rediscovered; Kings and Queens and Soup Tureens: The Campbell Museum Collection; The Circus in Art and Toys; and Guy Pene du Bois: The Twenties at Home and Abroad".

A new exhibit, guests, friends, patrons, artists...a preview is always an exhilarating evening. Wine, cheese, and hors d'oeuvres heighten the pleasure of the evening and are enjoyed by all in attendance.

John F. Francis (1808-1886)
Fruit and Wine, 1858
Oil on Canvas, 25 x 30 inches
Anonymous Gift

BARBECUED WATER CHESTNUTS

30 hors d'oeuvre

This is a great hors d'oeuvre that will disappear very quickly. It is a variation on rumaki for those who do not care for chicken livers.

1 (12-ounce) package
   thin sliced bacon
2 (8-ounce) cans water
   chestnuts, drained

1/2 cup packed brown
   sugar
1/4 cup chili sauce
1/2 cup mayonnaise

Preheat the oven to 350 degrees.

Cut each slice of bacon into 3 pieces; wrap each bacon piece around a water chestnut and secure with a wooden pick.

Arrange in a casserole. Bake at 350 degrees for 45 minutes or until the bacon is crisp. Drain well.

Combine the brown sugar, chili sauce and mayonnaise in a small bowl and blend well. Spoon over the bacon-wrapped water chestnuts. Bake for 15 minutes longer.

Arrange on a serving plate and serve immediately.
—*Doris Stillman*

The hors d'oeuvre is a rite rather than a course, and its duty is to enchant the eye, please the palate, and excite the flow of gastric juices...so that the meal to follow will seem doubly tempting and flavorful.
—James Beard (1903–1985)

PREVIEW NIGHT CHEESE SQUARES

80 canapés

Pass out this recipe to all who ask (and even those who don't!) This is a great recipe for holiday parties and unexpected guests. Keep some of the cheese mixture on hand in the refrigerator.

1 cup grated Parmesan
   cheese
1 cup finely shredded
   Swiss cheese
1 large red onion, minced
1½ cups mayonnaise
Salt to taste

20 slices firm white
   bread

Preheat the oven to 400 degrees.

Combine the Parmesan and Swiss cheeses, onion, mayonnaise and salt in a bowl and mix well.

Trim the crusts from the bread. Discard the crusts or reserve for another purpose. Spread the cheese mixture on the bread. Cut each bread slice into rectangular quarters. Place on a baking sheet.

Bake at 400 degrees for 10 to 12 minutes or until golden brown.

Serve hot or cold. —*Kathryn Chillingworth*

COCKTAIL SWIRLS

32 canapés

5 slices lean bacon
1 (8-ounce) container
   cream cheese with
   chives and onions,
   softened

1 (8-count) can crescent
   rolls
2 tablespoons (about)
   grated Parmesan
   cheese

Preheat the oven to 375 degrees.

Cook the bacon slices in microwave or skillet until crisp, drain on paper towels, cool and crumble. Combine the bacon with the cream cheese in a bowl and mix well by hand.

Separate the crescent roll dough into 4 rectangles. Spread the cream cheese mixture to the edges of the dough and roll each rectangle as for a jelly roll from the long side. Cut each roll into 8 pieces and arrange cut side down on an insulated baking sheet.

Bake at 375 degrees for 12 minutes or until golden brown. Remove from the oven and sprinkle with the Parmesan cheese. Let stand on the baking sheet for several minutes before removing carefully with a spatula.

These appetizers cannot be frozen but the cream cheese mixture may be prepared ahead.
—*Betty Henry*

PEANUT BUTTER AND BACON SQUARES

64 canapés

Another super-easy hors d'oeuvre for busy people. To prepare ahead, arrange the squares on the baking sheet, cover with waxed paper and refrigerate for several hours to a whole day. Broil just before serving and enjoy the compliments.

16 slices white sandwich
  bread
3/4 cup peanut butter
1/2 cup chili sauce
16 slices bacon

Preheat the broiler.

Place the bread slices on a baking sheet and broil until lightly toasted. Remove from the oven. Trim and discard the crusts.

Spread the peanut butter on the untoasted side of the bread. Spread the chili sauce over the peanut butter. Cut each bread slice into 4 squares.

Cut each slice of bacon into 4 pieces and place a bacon piece on top of each square.

Arrange the squares on a baking sheet. Broil until the bacon is crisp. Serve immediately.
—*Susan Bowman*

PINWHEEL HORS D'OEUVRE

64 hors d'oeuvre

A good accompaniment with drinks. The unsliced tortilla rolls may be refrigerated for several days before slicing to serve.

8 ounces cream cheese,
  softened
1 cup sour cream
1 (4-ounce) can chopped
  black olives, drained
1 (4-ounce) can chopped
  green chiles, drained
3 green onions, chopped
8 flour tortillas

Blend the cream cheese and sour cream in a small bowl.

Add the olives, green chiles and green onions and mix well.

Spread the mixture on each of the tortillas and roll tightly as for a jelly roll.

Wrap each roll individually in plastic wrap.

Wrap all 8 rolls in a wet towel and refrigerate for 8 hours or longer.

Slice each roll into 8 pieces and arrange on a serving plate. —*Eve Novak*

MARSALA MUSHROOMS

15 appetizer servings

This versatile recipe can be a delicious appetizer served hot or at room temperature. Good with almost any cut of beef, the mushrooms make an especially good sauce for beef fillet when the marsala is only slightly reduced.

2 tablespoons olive oil
2 tablespoons butter
1 large clove of garlic

2 pounds whole
   mushrooms

1 1/2 teaspoons instant
   bouillon
1 1/2 cups hot water
Cayenne to taste
1 1/2 cups marsala

Heat the olive oil and butter in a large skillet. Crush the garlic with the side of a large knife, keeping it in one piece. Add to the skillet and sauté for several minutes.

Wipe the mushrooms with a damp paper towel and trim only the stem ends. Add the mushrooms to the skillet and sauté for 15 minutes.

Remove and discard the garlic. Dissolve the bouillon in the hot water and pour over the mushrooms. Add the cayenne. Cook until most of the liquid has evaporated. Add the marsala.

Cook for 5 minutes or until the mushrooms are glazed, stirring frequently.

May prepare the mushrooms up to the point of adding the marsala and then let the mushrooms marinate in the marsala until just before serving time. Cook for 5 minutes or until glazed.
—*Jill Cook*

The sharpness and tingling aroma of raw garlic deepens, expands and softens when the garlic is heated.

MINIATURE REUBENS

24 canapés

This is a favorite at cocktail parties.

16 ounces refrigerated
    sauerkraut
Russian Dressing
    (see below)
24 slices party rye or
    pumpernickel bread
8 ounces corned beef,
    thinly sliced
8 ounces Swiss cheese,
    sliced

Drain the sauerkraut well and chop finely. Mix with ½ cup of the dressing.

Arrange the bread slices on a lightly greased baking sheet.

Fold or cut the corned beef slices to fit the bread slices and place on the bread. Spread 1 teaspoon of the sauerkraut mixture on each of the corned beef slices.

Top with Swiss cheese slices that have been trimmed to fit the bread.

Arrange on a baking sheet and store, tightly covered, in the refrigerator until almost serving time. Preheat the oven to 325 degrees.

Bake the Reubens at 325 degrees for 10 minutes or just until the cheese starts to melt.

Reubens may be frozen before baking, if tightly wrapped in plastic wrap and foil. Allow to thaw before baking.

RUSSIAN DRESSING

¾ cup

½ cup mayonnaise
¼ cup chili sauce
1½ teaspoons
    horseradish

Combine the mayonnaise, chili sauce and horseradish in a small bowl and mix well.

Store, covered, in the refrigerator.
—*Gladys M. Waugaman*

Aya stova on or Kitchen stove great place - pool, heated floor -

HERBED ZUCCHINI SQUARES

40 hors d'oeuvre

This is a light and very uniquely flavored hors d'oeuvre.

1 cup egg substitute
1/4 teaspoon rosemary, finely crushed
1/8 teaspoon thyme
1/8 teaspoon basil
1/2 teaspoon salt
1/4 teaspoon white pepper
1 tablespoon Sambuca

1 1/2 cups low-fat baking mix
1/2 teaspoon cream of tartar
2/3 cup chopped red onion
1 large clove of garlic, minced
2 tablespoons chopped chives
1 tablespoon chopped cilantro
1 tablespoon chopped banana pepper

1/2 cup extra-virgin olive oil
3 cups quartered sliced zucchini

Preheat the oven to 350 degrees.

Mix the egg substitute, rosemary, thyme, basil, salt and pepper in a small bowl. Add the Sambuca; mix well.

Combine the baking mix, cream of tartar, red onion, garlic, chives, cilantro and banana pepper in a large bowl; mix well.

Add the egg substitute and herb mixture and olive oil; mix well. Fold in the sliced zucchini.

Pour into a 9x13-inch baking pan coated with nonstick cooking spray.

Bake at 350 degrees for 30 minutes or until light brown.

Let stand for several minutes before cutting. Cut into squares and arrange on a decorative plate. Serve the zucchini squares warm.

May substitute your own favorite combination of herbs. —*Robert Walsh*

ARTICHOKE CHEESE SPREAD

32 servings

Serve Artichoke Cheese Spread as a simple, quickly prepared appetizer with your favorite crackers. Or serve with toast points for lunch.

1 cup mayonnaise
1½ to 2 cups shredded
  Cheddar cheese
1 (12-ounce) can
  artichokes, drained,
  chopped

Preheat the oven to 350 degrees.

Combine the mayonnaise and shredded Cheddar cheese in a medium bowl and mix well. Stir in the artichokes and spoon the mixture into a baking pan.

Bake at 350 degrees for 20 minutes.

May substitute grated Parmesan cheese for the shredded Cheddar cheese.

As a variation, add one 10-ounce package thawed frozen chopped spinach, squeezed dry, or one 4-ounce jar chopped green chiles or add a small can of drained crab meat. —*Catharine Celli*

BLEU CHEESE LOVER'S DELIGHT

12 servings

Easy to make, and easy to prepare in advance.

8 ounces bleu cheese,
  softened
8 ounces cream cheese,
  softened
Worcestershire sauce to
  taste
Tabasco sauce to taste
Paprika to taste

Blend the bleu cheese and cream cheese with a fork in a small bowl. Add the Worcestershire sauce, Tabasco sauce and paprika; mix well.

Spoon into a serving bowl. Chill until time to serve. Serve with assorted crackers.

May substitute Roquefort cheese for the bleu cheese. —*Doris Springer*

CAPONATA

20 servings

This tasty recipe is best if prepared at least one day before serving.

1 (1-pound) unpeeled
  eggplant
1 medium onion
1/2 cup chopped green
  bell pepper
2 to 3 cloves of garlic,
  chopped
8 ounces mushrooms,
  sliced
1/3 cup olive oil

2 (6-ounce) cans tomato
  paste
1/4 cup water
2 tablespoons wine
  vinegar
2 teaspoons sugar
1/2 cup chopped black
  olives
3 to 4 tablespoons pine
  nuts
1/2 teaspoon oregano
1 teaspoon salt
1/2 teaspoon pepper

Chop the eggplant into fine pieces; place in a bowl. Chop the onion; add to the eggplant.

Combine the eggplant, onion, green pepper, garlic and mushrooms and add to the olive oil in a skillet. Simmer, covered, for 10 to 15 minutes.

Add the tomato paste, water, wine vinegar, sugar, black olives, nuts, oregano, salt and pepper; mix well. Simmer, covered, for 15 minutes. Remove the cover; simmer for 15 minutes longer.

Spoon into a bowl and chill, covered, for 24 hours or longer for best results.

Serve with crackers or small slices of rye bread.
—*Audrey Stern*

Let eggplant serve both as an ingredient and as a container for the chilled appetizer. Scoop the pulp and seeds from 1/2 of an eggplant and spoon the caponata into the shell for an attractive presentation.

HOT CRAB DIP

24 servings

8 ounces Nuefchâtel
   cheese, softened
1 teaspoon dried onion
½ teaspoon prepared
   horseradish
¼ teaspoon salt
White pepper to taste
1 (6-ounce) can lump
   crab meat, drained
½ cup blanched slivered
   almonds

Combine the cheese with the onion, horseradish, salt and white pepper in a small bowl. Stir in the crab meat; mix well.

Spoon the mixture into a small baking dish. Sprinkle with the blanched almonds.

Bake at 370 degrees for 20 to 30 minutes or until bubbly. Serve hot with party rye or pumpernickel bread.

May substitute cream cheese for the Nuefchâtel cheese. —*Joan DeRose*

JAVA NUT BRIE

12 servings

This recipe is superb as an appetizer for a large cocktail event and also makes an unusual dessert for a small dinner party.

¾ cup finely chopped
   pecans
¼ cup Kahlúa
3 tablespoons brown
   sugar

1 (14-ounce) wheel of
   Brie cheese

Spread the chopped pecans in a 9-inch glass pie plate. Microwave on High for 4 to 6 minutes or until the pecans are toasted. Add the liqueur and brown sugar; mix well.

Remove the top rind of the cheese. Place the cheese in the center of the pie plate, spooning the pecan mixture over the top.

Microwave on High for 1 to 2 minutes or just until the cheese is slightly softened.

Serve with apple slices, crackers, melba toast or gingersnaps. —*Johny DeRose*

CURRIED SHRIMP DIP

20 servings

8 ounces cream cheese,
  softened
2 tablespoons
  mayonnaise
1/2 teaspoon (or more)
  curry powder
Salt and white pepper to
  taste
1 (6-ounce) can tiny
  shrimp
1 small stalk celery with
  leaves, finely chopped
1 tablespoon minced
  scallion
2 teaspoons lemon juice
1 hard-cooked egg,
  grated
Chopped parsley to taste

Blend the cream cheese with the mayonnaise, curry powder, salt and white pepper in a small bowl.

Drain the shrimp well. Devein and finely chop the shrimp. Toss with the celery, scallion and lemon juice.

Spoon the cream cheese mixture into a shallow serving dish such as a decorative pie plate.

Sprinkle the shrimp mixture over the top. Top with the egg and parsley.

Serve with tortilla chips or small crisp crackers.
—*Isabel Haggerson*

SMOKEY APPETIZER PÂTÉ

20 servings

This is striking served on a black plate.

8 ounces smoked trout
8 ounces cream cheese,
  softened
1/2 cup sour cream
1 tablespoon pepper
Paprika to taste

Process the trout in a food processor container until finely chopped. Add the cream cheese, sour cream and pepper. Process until smooth.

Spread the mixture in a circle on a serving plate. Sprinkle with paprika. Chill until serving time.

Serve with crisp unsalted crackers.

May substitute smoked turkey or bluefish for the trout. —*Marquis Smith III*

PERKY TEX-MEX DIP

20 servings

Men love this!

2 cups sour cream
2 envelopes taco
   seasoning mix
Chili powder to taste

2 (10-ounce) cans
   jalapeño bean dip
2 bunches scallions,
   thinly sliced
1 (4-ounce) can chopped
   black olives
2 large tomatoes,
   seeded, chopped
2 cups shredded
   Cheddar cheese

Combine the sour cream, taco seasoning and chili powder in a small bowl; mix well.

Spread the bean dip on a large serving platter. Layer the sour cream mixture, scallions, black olives and tomatoes over the bean dip. Sprinkle the Cheddar cheese over the top.

Chill in the refrigerator. Serve with tortilla chips or corn chips.

May substitute shredded Monterey Jack cheese for the shredded Cheddar cheese. —*Barbara Jamison*

Garnish an hors d'oeuvre tray with ham and pickle rounds. Spread 1 pound baked or boiled ham slices with 8 ounces softened cream cheese. Arrange a whole dill pickle (found in the refrigerated deli section) in the center of each slice. Roll to enclose the pickle. Chill for several hours to overnight. Slice into ¼-inch rounds.

SEAFOOD SALSA WITH CHIPS

28 servings

Perfect for an open house, this is an appetizer with a very refreshing taste.

1/2 pound bay scallops
1/2 pound fresh lump
  crab meat, drained
1/2 cup fresh lime juice
1 teaspoon grated
  tangerine rind

2/3 cup chopped tangerine
1/2 cup chopped peeled,
  seeded tomato
2 tablespoons finely
  chopped purple onion
1 tablespoon chopped
  fresh cilantro
1 tablespoon minced
  fresh jalapeño
1/8 teaspoon salt

Cook the scallops in a nonstick skillet over medium heat for about 3 minutes; drain. Combine the scallops with the crab meat, lime juice and tangerine rind in a bowl. Chill, covered, until serving time.

Mix the tangerine, tomato, purple onion, cilantro, jalapeño and salt in a small bowl. Chill, covered, until serving time.

Stir the tangerine mixture into the scallop mixture just before serving. Spoon into a serving dish. Garnish with fresh cilantro leaves.

Serve the salsa with the Baked Tortilla Chips (see below).

BAKED TORTILLA CHIPS

7 (6-inch) corn tortillas

Preheat the oven to 350 degrees.

Cut each tortilla into 8 wedges and arrange in a single layer on a baking sheet.

Bake at 350 degrees for 10 minutes or until crisp. Let cool.

Store the wedges in an airtight container.
—*Summer Friedlander*

WIDOWER'S HORS D'OEUVRE

10 servings

1/2 cup freshly grated
  horseradish
1 cup whipping cream,
  whipped
1/2 envelope unflavored
  gelatin
1/4 cup milk

Fold the horseradish gently into the whipped cream in a small bowl.

Soften the gelatin in the milk in a microwave-safe dish. Microwave on High for 1 minute. Stir until the gelatin dissolves.

Stir the gelatin mixture into the whipped cream mixture. Chill until set.

Serve on crackers thinly spread with creamy peanut butter. —*Annette Rathbun*

CURRY DIP FOR VEGETABLES

1 cup

3/4 cup mayonnaise
2 tablespoons Durkee
  sauce
1 teaspoon horseradish
1 teaspoon celery seeds
1 teaspoon curry powder
1/2 teaspoon salt
1/4 teaspoon
  Worcestershire sauce
Tabasco sauce to taste
Pepper to taste

Combine the mayonnaise, Durkee sauce, horseradish, celery seeds, curry powder, salt, Worcestershire sauce, Tabasco sauce and pepper in a bowl; mix well.

Chill for 1 hour or longer.

Serve with assorted fresh vegetables and crisp crackers. —*Sally Loughran*

Serve this hors d'oeuvre in a garden of color in hollowed-out whole red, green or orange bell peppers. Surround your servings with blanched green beans, broccoli florets, slices of red and yellow bell peppers, carrot strips and celery sticks for dipping. A hollowed-out red cabbage also makes an attractive container.

CHINESE FRIED WALNUTS

4 cups

Since these nuts can be prepared up to two weeks in advance, they make a nice gift at Christmas. Place the sweet nuts in decorated containers such as jam jars.

6 cups water
4 cups walnut halves
½ cup sugar
Salt to taste
Vegetable oil for frying

Bring the water to a boil in a 4-quart saucepan. Add the walnuts. Bring to a boil. Cook for 1 minute. Rinse the walnuts under hot running water; drain.

Combine the warm nuts with the sugar in a bowl; mix well. Let stand for 5 minutes or until the sugar has dissolved.

Heat 1 inch oil in a skillet to 350 degrees on a cooking thermometer.

Fry the walnuts ½ at a time for 5 minutes or until golden brown, stirring frequently. Remove the walnuts with a slotted spoon.

Drain the walnuts in a sieve over a bowl. Sprinkle lightly with salt; toss to separate.

Spread in a single layer on paper towels. Let stand until cool.

Store in an airtight container. —*Sue Pollins*

For quick endive stuffers spread one of these mixtures on the stem end of endive spears for a great hors d'oeuvre: peanut butter and chutney; or cream cheese, mayonnaise, curry powder and chopped canned shrimp. Arrange the stuffed endive in concentric circles, by filling and by size, on a serving plate.

SUGAR-AND-SPICE PECANS

2 cups

Are you looking for a bridge club snack that's a little different? If so, try these spicy treats. Or serve as a dessert with after-dinner coffee.

1/2 cup sugar
1 teaspoon cinnamon
1/4 teaspoon nutmeg
1/4 teaspoon ground
  cloves
3/4 teaspoon salt
1 egg white
2 tablespoons orange
  juice
2 cups shelled pecans

Preheat the oven to 300 degrees.

Combine the sugar, cinnamon, nutmeg, cloves and salt in a bowl; mix well.

Beat the egg white in a bowl until frothy. Add the orange juice; mix well. Stir in the pecans; toss to moisten. Sprinkle the sugar mixture over the pecans. Place the pecans in one layer on a nonstick baking sheet sprayed with nonstick cooking spray.

Bake at 300 degrees for 25 to 30 minutes or until golden brown. Cool. Remove the pecans with a spatula carefully. Store in an airtight container.
—*Joan DeRose*

POWER PUNCH

30 servings

This is a very potent punch, but absolutely delicious!

2 lemons, thinly sliced
1 (8-ounce) jar
  maraschino cherries

1 1/2 cups sugar
2 pints fresh lemon juice
1 3/5 quarts Jamaican
  light rum
2 pints Cognac
2 quarts club soda
4 ounces peach liqueur

Place the sliced lemons and cherries in a small ring mold; fill with water. Freeze until solid. Unmold the ring when ready to serve the punch.

Dissolve the sugar in the lemon juice in a large punch bowl. Add the rum, brandy, club soda and liqueur; mix well.

Chill for 2 hours; stir at intervals. Place the lemon and cherry ice ring on top to serve. —*Lee Wood*

CHAMPAGNE PUNCH

24 servings

1 pineapple, trimmed,
   peeled, finely cubed
1/4 cup sugar
1/2 cup lemon juice
1/2 cup water
1 cup sugar
3 bottles Champagne,
   chilled
1 bottle sauterne
1 quart sparkling water,
   chilled

Combine the pineapple with the 1/4 cup sugar in a bowl; toss to coat. Place 1 cup of the sweetened pineapple in a ring mold. Chill the remaining pineapple for 8 hours to overnight.

Fill the mold with water; freeze until firm.

Mix the lemon juice, water and 1 cup sugar in a bowl; chill.

Spoon the chilled pineapple and the lemon juice mixture into a large punch bowl. Add the Champagne, sauterne and sparkling water; mix well.

Add the pineapple ice ring just before serving.
—*Joan DeRose*

RUBY PUNCH

50 servings

2²/3 cups lemon juice
1/2 cup sugar
6 quarts white grape
   juice, chilled
6 quarts ginger ale,
   chilled
3 quarts cranberry juice,
   chilled

Combine the lemon juice and sugar in a pitcher. Chill for 6 to 8 hours. Pour into a punch bowl.

Add the white grape juice, ginger ale and cranberry juice to the lemon mixture just before serving; mix well.

Garnish with an ice ring and thin lemon slices.

May substitute 8 liters dry Champagne for the white grape juice; add brandy if desired.
—**Art In The Kitchen** *Cookbook Committee*

TEAS, LECTURES, AND LUNCHEONS

Being asked "to pour the tea" has always been considered an honor. Part of the gentle art espoused by many cultures, the duties were left to the women. In 1960, forty Greensburg women were invited to form the Women's Committee of the Westmoreland Museum of Art. Acting as hostesses at Museum functions, we set elaborate tea tables, baked cookies, and arranged flowers. Wearing party dresses, white gloves, and hats, we took turns pouring tea, greeting guests, and being runners to replenish the trays.

During the past 35 years, our mission and membership enlarged; our activities evolved to focus on education and fund-raising. We sponsor annually a luncheon lecture series, the "Art in Bloom" exhibition, Children's Day, a seasonal gala, and the preview party for the holiday toy exhibit. Funds raised by our efforts purchase additions to the permanent collection, and since 1993, our members have managed the Museum Store. *Art in the Kitchen* is our first publication. The book's preparation and recipe testing gave opportunity to savor many museum memories and to renew our dedication to welcome both old and new friends to the museum.

Cecilia Beaux (1855-1942)
Still Life with Fruit, c. 1918
Oil on Canvas, 24 1/4 x 18 inches
Gift of the Women's Committee

SPINACH AND SUN-DRIED TOMATO CALZONE

12 servings

This recipe can be easily adapted to serve as an appetizer, a full-course luncheon or a party snack.

1 (10-ounce) package
    frozen spinach
1 package pizza crust
    mix
1/2 teaspoon garlic
    powder
8 ounces bacon,
    crisp-fried, crumbled
8 ounces mozzarella,
    sliced
1/2 cup sun-dried
    tomatoes
1 egg white, beaten
1 teaspoon sesame seeds

Preheat the oven to 350 degrees.

Cook the spinach using package directions; drain well and squeeze dry.

Prepare the pizza crust mix using package directions. Pat into a greased round pizza pan or onto a greased baking sheet. Sprinkle with the garlic powder.

Alternate layers of bacon, cheese, spinach and sun-dried tomatoes on half the crust until all the ingredients are used. Carefully fold the other half of the crust over the top and seal the edges. Brush with egg white and sprinkle with sesame seeds.

Bake at 350 degrees for 20 minutes or until golden brown. Remove the calzone from the oven and let stand for 10 to 15 minutes before serving.

May substitute frozen broccoli, pepperoni and Velveeta cheese or different cheeses for the filling.

The calzone may be frozen after baking, then reheated and served at a later time.
—*Rose D. Mack*

Queen Anne Cucumber Sandwiches

30 canapés

A 90s update of a classic tea sandwich.

1 tablespoon mayonnaise
8 ounces cream cheese, softened
1 envelope Italian salad dressing mix
1/8 teaspoon lemon juice

30 slices party pumpernickel bread
1 cucumber, thinly sliced
Dillweed to taste

Combine the mayonnaise and cream cheese in a small mixer bowl and beat until smooth. Add the salad dressing mix and lemon juice and blend well.

Spread the mayonnaise mixture on one side of each bread slice. Top with 1 slice of cucumber and a sprinkle of dillweed.

May substitute 30 slices party rye bread for pumpernickel bread. —*Debbie Reese*

Hot Ham and Cheese Sandwiches

16 sandwiches

6 tablespoons mayonnaise
1 cup chili sauce
2/3 cup finely chopped onion
4 hard-cooked eggs, diced
1 cup cubed sharp Cheddar cheese
1 cup chopped pimento-stuffed green olives
1 cup cubed baked ham
16 sandwich buns, split

Preheat the oven to 400 degrees.

Blend the mayonnaise and chili sauce in a medium bowl. Add the onion, eggs, cheese, olives and ham and mix well.

Spread the ham mixture on the bottom slice of each bun. Cover with the top of the bun. Wrap the sandwiches individually in foil and place on a large baking sheet.

Bake at 400 degrees for 10 to 15 minutes. Unwrap and serve immediately.

The sandwiches may be chilled or frozen after wrapping in foil. Allow the sandwiches to come to room temperature before baking or if frozen bake for several minutes longer until heated through. —*Jean K. Wilcox*

RED PEPPER AND SPINACH BISQUES

16 servings

Red Pepper Bisque
  (see below)
Spinach Bisque
  (see below)
3 cups heavy cream
16 small Brie wedges
Reduced cream

Stir enough cream into each bisque to obtain a smooth but thick consistency. Cook just until heated through. Be sure that both bisques are of the same consistency so each will maintain its own space in the bowl.

Ladle each bisque at the same time into opposite sides of warm soup plates. Garnish each with a small wedge of Brie or drizzle of reduced cream.

RED PEPPER BISQUE

2 tablespoons butter
1/2 cup chopped onion
1/2 cup chopped shallot
1 cup chopped celery
1 cup chopped carrots
1 cup chopped peeled
  potato
3 quarts chicken or
  vegetable stock
12 red peppers, roasted,
  peeled
Salt and pepper to taste

Melt the butter in a large saucepan. Stir in the onion, shallot, celery, carrots and potato. Cook over medium heat until onion is tender. Add the stock and red peppers. Bring to a boil; reduce the heat. Simmer for 30 minutes; cool. Purée the mixture through a strainer or sieve into a large bowl. Return the mixture to the large saucepan.

Reduce further to obtain a thick consistency or thicken with a roux. Add salt and pepper to taste. Keep warm until serving time.

SPINACH BISQUE

2 tablespoons butter
1/2 cup chopped onion
2 cloves of garlic, minced
1 cup chopped celery
1/2 cup chopped carrot
1 cup chopped peeled
  potato
3 quarts chicken or
  vegetable stock
2 to 3 pounds fresh
  spinach
Salt and pepper to taste
Nutmeg to taste

Melt the butter in a large saucepan. Stir in the onion, garlic, celery, carrot and potato. Cook over medium heat until the onion is tender. Add the stock. Rinse and drain the spinach. Add to the stock mixture and bring to a boil. Reduce the heat and simmer for 30 minutes. Purée the mixture through a strainer or sieve into a large bowl. Return the puréed mixture to the large saucepan.

Reduce further to obtain a thick consistency. Add salt, pepper and nutmeg to taste. Keep warm until serving time.

—*Linda Earnest*, **The Earnest Gourmet**

Avgolémono

6 servings

Avgolémono is pronounced "ah-vwo-lém-o-no". (You know, the Greeks always have a word for it!) Avgolémono is an easy-to-prepare, nutritious and inexpensive Greek soup with a wonderful lemon taste. This recipe has been handed down by many generations of Greek cooks in my family, including my grandmother, my aunts and my mother. To paraphrase Socrates, speaking from the Lyceum in Athens, this recipe is "food for the gods" being shared with the Westmoreland Museum.

1 quart chicken broth
½ cup uncooked rice
2 eggs, beaten
Juice of 1 lemon

Pour the chicken broth into a medium saucepan. Stir the rice into the broth and bring to a boil. Reduce heat. Cook, covered, until the rice is tender.

Beat the eggs with the lemon juice. Stir gradually a small amount of the hot rice mixture into the egg mixture. Stir gradually the eggs into the hot mixture.

Ladle into soup bowls and garnish with parsley sprigs.

May prepare the soup ahead and keep warm over hot but not boiling water. —*Elaine Bryan*

The discovery of a new dish does more for the happiness of mankind than the discovery of a new star. —Brillat Savarin (1755–1826)

CHICKEN SALAD WITH CURRY DRESSING

10 servings

Curried chicken as a salad features 5-boy condiments and chutney mixed right in.

5 cups chopped cooked
  chicken
2 cups sliced grapes
1 cup chopped celery
½ cup slivered almonds
½ cup sliced green
  onions
½ (8-ounce) can water
  chestnuts

1 cup sour cream
1 cup mayonnaise
¼ cup chopped chutney
1 teaspoon curry powder

Combine the chicken, grapes, celery, almonds, green onions and water chestnuts in a large bowl; mix well.

Blend the sour cream and mayonnaise together in a small bowl. Add the chutney and curry powder, stirring until well blended.

Spoon the sour cream mixture over the chicken mixture, and mix gently.

Chill, covered, until ready to serve.

May substitute 2 cups drained pineapple tidbits for the grapes. —*Virginia Grosscup*

Start a picture-perfect summer brunch with cold melon soup. Purée 1½ cups each of cantaloupe and honeydew with 2 cups orange juice and 3 tablespoons honey. Add 2 cups dry Champagne and 1½ cups each chopped cantaloupe and honeydew. Serve the soup well chilled.

R.B.'s Chicken Salad

16 servings

A honey and mustard dressing updates this chicken salad.

3 quarts water
1 large onion, cut into
    quarters
1 stalk celery
3 sprigs of parsley
10 peppercorns
6 chicken breasts halves
12 chicken thighs

4 large stalks celery,
    finely chopped
1½ cups red grape
    halves
1½ cups green grape
    halves
12 ounces Cheddar
    cheese, cubed

1½ cups mayonnaise
½ cup sour cream
¼ cup honey
1 tablespoon Dijon
    mustard
Salt and pepper to taste

Bring the water to a boil in a large stockpot. Add the onion, celery stalk, parsley and peppercorns; mix well. Rinse the chicken and add to the stockpot. Reduce the heat and simmer for 15 to 20 minutes or until the chicken is tender. Cool in the stockpot for 15 minutes.

Remove the chicken. Cut the chicken into bite-size pieces, discarding the skin and bones.

Combine the chopped celery, grape halves and cheese cubes in a large bowl. Add the chicken and mix lightly.

Blend the mayonnaise and sour cream in a small bowl. Stir in the honey in a fine stream and add the mustard. Pour over the chicken mixture and mix lightly until coated. Add salt and pepper to taste. Garnish with parsley.

Do not substitute light mayonnaise for mayonnaise since doing so may affect the consistency of the salad.

May substitute Jarlsburg cheese for Cheddar cheese or substitute additional chicken breasts for the chicken thighs if all white meat is preferred.
—*Robert B. Weidlein*
Huntland Farm Bed & Breakfast

ELEGANT GARDEN PASTA SALAD

12 servings

Serve this centerpiece salad on a large green platter for a truly elegant presentation.

16 ounces fettuccine, cooked
1 (16-ounce) package frozen green peas
1½ pounds cooked peeled shrimp
3 cups cherry tomato halves
1 cup chopped red or yellow bell peppers
1 cup chopped scallions
1 cup artichoke heart quarter
4 cloves of garlic, minced
1 medium onion, finely chopped
Garden Pasta Salad Dressing (see below)

Cook the pasta in boiling water to cover. Cook the peas in a saucepan according to package directions; drain.

Combine the fettuccine and shrimp in a large bowl. Add the peas, tomatoes, peppers, scallions, artichoke hearts, garlic and onion, tossing lightly to mix.

Chill in the refrigerator.

Pour the Garden Pasta Salad Dressing over the pasta mixture and toss lightly. Cover and chill until ready to serve.

GARDEN PASTA SALAD DRESSING

½ cup chicken broth
¼ cup olive oil
¼ cup cider vinegar
1½ cups pesto sauce
1½ teaspoons Dijon mustard
1 teaspoon Tabasco sauce
½ cup minced parsley
2 tablespoons minced fresh oregano
3 tablespoons sugar
1½ teaspoons salt
Pepper to taste

Combine the broth, olive oil, vinegar, pesto sauce, mustard and Tabasco sauce in a medium bowl; mix until well blended.

Stir in the parsley, oregano, sugar, salt and pepper.
—*Melissa Rodgers*

HORSERADISH AND TOMATO ASPIC

6 servings

A unique, tangy aspic will stand out from the rest, try this easy recipe.

1 (3-ounce) package
  lemon gelatin
1¼ cups boiling water
1 (8-ounce) can tomato
  sauce
1¼ tablespoons white
  wine vinegar
2 tablespoons
  horseradish
½ teaspoon salt
Dash of pepper

Dissolve the gelatin in the boiling water in a medium bowl. Stir in the tomato sauce, vinegar, horseradish, salt and pepper.

Pour into a mold. Chill, covered, until firm.

Unmold the aspic onto a lettuce-lined serving plate. May substitute white wine for the white wine vinegar. —*Kathryn Jamison*

SALMON AND DILL MOLD

6 servings

A fish-shaped mold is attractive for this recipe. Serve with French bread or bagel chips for an hors d'oeuvre.

8 ounces cream cheese,
  softened
2 tablespoons sour cream
1 cup flaked cooked
  salmon
¼ cup chopped red bell
  pepper
¼ cup chopped celery
¼ cup chopped green
  onions
1 teaspoon fresh dill
1 teaspoon Tabasco
  sauce
1 teaspoon horseradish

Blend the cream cheese and sour cream in a large bowl.

Add the salmon, red pepper, celery, green onions, dill, Tabasco sauce and horseradish; mix well.

Spoon into a greased mold.

Chill, covered, for 2 hours.

Unmold onto a serving plate. —*Cicely Gilbert*

TOMATO AND RASPBERRY MOLD

24 servings

A gelatin mold with zip, this tangy salad has been served at Art in Bloom luncheons.

3 (3-ounce) packages
  raspberry gelatin
1½ cups boiling water
2 (16-ounce) cans
  tomatoes
10 drops of hot pepper
  sauce

½ cup sour cream
½ cup mayonnaise
1 teaspoon (or more)
  horseradish
1 teaspoon sugar
Salt to taste

Dissolve the gelatin in boiling water in a large bowl.

Purée the undrained tomatoes in a blender. Remove any pieces of the cores. Add the tomatoes to the gelatin mixture and stir in the hot pepper sauce. Pour the mixture into a 9x13-inch glass dish or other attractive dish or mold.

Chill, covered, until firm.

Unmold onto a serving plate if desired.

Blend the sour cream and mayonnaise in a small bowl. Add the horseradish, sugar and salt; blend until smooth. Thin the topping with a small amount of milk for easier drizzling if necessary.

Drizzle the sour cream topping over the entire mold before serving or add a dollop of the topping to individual servings. —*Joan DeRose*

CHICKEN AND LEMON MOUSSE

6 servings

Perfect for a luncheon or buffet served with fresh asparagus and flaky croissants..

2 cups chicken broth
1 (3-ounce) package
   lemon gelatin
2 tablespoons white
   wine vinegar
1/2 teaspoon salt
2 cups finely chopped
   celery
3 cups chopped cooked
   chicken breasts
1 (2-ounce) jar pimentos
1 cup whipping cream

Bring the broth to a boil in a medium saucepan. Dissolve the gelatin in the boiling broth.

Stir in the vinegar and salt. Pour into a medium mixer bowl.

Chill until the gelatin is partially congealed.

Beat the gelatin mixture in the mixer bowl until frothy. Fold in the celery, chicken and pimentos.

Whip the whipping cream in a mixer bowl until soft peaks form.

Fold the whipped cream gently into the gelatin mixture with a rubber spatula, rotating the bowl 1/4 turn after each motion. Spoon into a mold.

Chill, covered, until set.

Unmold onto a serving plate. —*Ruth Cook*

SHRIMP MOUSSE

20 servings

Use a fish-shaped mold for this delicious mousse.

1 (10-ounce) can tomato
    soup
8 ounces cream cheese,
    softened
1½ envelopes
    unflavored gelatin
½ cup cold water
1 cup mayonnaise
1 cup chopped celery
½ cup chopped green
    bell pepper
½ cup chopped onion
1 pound shrimp, cooked,
    peeled, chopped
Seasoned salt to taste
Parsley to taste
Hot pepper sauce to taste
2 tablespoons
    mayonnaise

Cook the soup and cream cheese in a large saucepan over low heat until the cream cheese melts and the mixture is smooth, stirring constantly.

Soften the gelatin in the cold water. Add to the cream cheese mixture, stirring until the gelatin dissolves completely.

Remove the cream cheese mixture from the heat and blend in 1 cup mayonnaise.

Mix in the celery, green pepper and onion.

Stir in the shrimp; add seasoned salt, parsley and hot pepper sauce to taste.

Coat the inside of a mold lightly with 2 tablespoons mayonnaise. Spoon the mousse mixture into the mold.

Chill, covered, for 3 hours or until firm.

Unmold the mousse onto a serving plate. Decorate with cucumber, green olives and pimento.
—*Sheryl K. Wolf*

For an artistic addition to a salad buffet, be creative in decorating the mousse. Overlap layers of thinly sliced cucumbers on the mousse to resemble fish scales. Use pimento-stuffed green olive slices for the eyes.

TUNA MOUSSE

20 servings

1 envelope unflavored
  gelatin
¼ cup cold water
2 cups mayonnaise
4 teaspoons tarragon
  vinegar
½ teaspoon salt
2 tablespoons sweet
  relish
1 cup chopped celery
¾ cup chopped
  pimento-stuffed green
  olives
4 hard-cooked eggs,
  chopped
2 (6-ounce) cans white
  tuna, drained, flaked

Soften the gelatin in the cold water. Heat in a double boiler over simmering water until gelatin dissolves. Cool to room temperature.

Whisk the mayonnaise, vinegar and salt into the gelatin. Fold in the relish, celery, olives, eggs and tuna.

Spoon the mixture into a lightly greased ring mold. Cover and chill until firm.

Unmold onto a serving plate.

May easily double the recipe. —*Eleanor Smith*

Make decorative citrus cups by cutting oranges, lemons or limes into halves and scooping out the pulp. Cut edges into scallops or zigzag if you wish. Fill the shells with fruit salad, molded salad or cranberry relish.

58

ZESTY MANDARIN ORANGE SALAD

6 servings

1 (11-ounce) can
  mandarin oranges
1 head lettuce, torn into
  bite-size pieces
1/2 small mild white
  onion, sliced into rings
1 cup chopped celery
Walnut Dressing or
  Almond Dressing
  (see below)

Drain the mandarin oranges, reserving the juice if using with the walnut dressing.

Combine the lettuce, mandarin oranges, onion and celery in a large salad bowl.

Pour the desired dressing over the lettuce mixture, tossing to coat.

May omit the celery.

WALNUT DRESSING

1 1/2 tablespoons butter
1/4 teaspoon salt
2/3 cup chopped walnuts

1/2 cup cider vinegar
1 cup sugar
1/2 teaspoon salt
1/2 teaspoon dry mustard
1/2 teaspoon paprika
1 tablespoon celery seeds
Juice of 1/2 onion
1 cup vegetable oil
Mandarin orange juice

Melt the butter in a small saucepan over medium heat. Add the salt and walnuts. Sauté until the walnuts are crisp, stirring frequently. Set aside to cool.

Beat the vinegar, sugar, salt, dry mustard, paprika, celery seeds and onion juice in a mixer bowl. Add the oil in a fine stream, beating constantly. Add enough mandarin orange juice to make of the desired consistency. Sprinkle walnuts on top.

May substitute chopped pecans for the walnuts.
—*Joan DeRose*

ALMOND DRESSING

1/2 cup salad oil
2 tablespoons malt
  vinegar
2 tablespoons sugar
1/4 teaspoon salt
1/8 teaspoon almond
  extract

Combine the oil, vinegar, sugar, salt and almond flavoring in a small bowl, blending well.
—*Susan Bowman*

MONET'S GARDEN SALAD

6 servings

A tribute to Monet's color-suffused garden impressions, this salad is a mingling of color and textures. Create your own impressions with your favorite salad greens, such as arugula, Boston lettuce and nasturtium or basil leaves. Choose any fresh herbs—thyme, lemon thyme, tarragon or oregano leaves. Nasturtiums add a unique peppery taste. Grow your own nasturtiums—pretty flowers that are easy to raise and bloom profusely until the first frost.

1 head red leaf lettuce
1 head green leaf lettuce
Salad greens of choice
Large double handful of
 nasturtium flowers
Large handful of thyme
 flowers

1/2 red bell pepper
1/2 yellow bell pepper
1 tablespoon lemon juice
1 tablespoon olive oil
1/2 cup sliced fresh
 mushrooms
Fresh herbs of choice
Vinaigrette Dressing
 (see below)

Rinse the leaf lettuce, salad greens and flowers. Drain. Roll up in paper towels to dry until serving time.

Slice the bell peppers into thin 1/4-inch strips, discarding the seeds and membranes. Sprinkle lemon juice and olive oil on mushrooms.

Combine the lettuce, greens, mushrooms, bell peppers and herbs in a large serving bowl.

Scatter the thyme flowers and nasturtiums over the top of the salad. Whole cherry tomatoes may be arranged around the perimeter of salad bowl.

Add the Vinaigrette Dressing and toss well just before serving.

VINAIGRETTE DRESSING

1 small clove of garlic,
 crushed
1/4 teaspoon salt
1/4 teaspoon freshly
 ground pepper
2 teaspoons freshly
 squeezed lemon juice
1 tablespoon red wine
 vinegar
4 to 5 tablespoons
 extra-virgin olive oil

Place the garlic in a mortar. Add the salt and pepper. Pound with a pestle until the salt is pulverized and the garlic is a purée.

Add the lemon juice, vinegar and olive oil, stirring constantly.

May substitute 1 teaspoon mixed dried herbs and 1/4 teaspoon Dijon mustard for the garlic.
—Linda Austin

SPINACH AND BACON SALAD

8 servings

The thin, tangy dressing is slightly sweet. You may prefer serving this crisp green salad European-style—as a separate course after the entrêe.

2 pounds fresh spinach
2 heads red leaf lettuce
8 slices bacon

¹/₃ cup cider vinegar
1 cup vegetable oil
1 tablespoon onion juice
1 teaspoon salt
1 teaspoon dry mustard
1 tablespoon poppy
   seeds
1¹/₂ cups large curd
   cottage cheese

Rinse the spinach and red leaf lettuce and pat dry. Discard stems and tear the leaves into bite-size pieces. Place the spinach and lettuce in a large salad bowl.

Fry the bacon and drain on paper towels. Pat bacon strips dry and crumble. Add the bacon to the lettuce mixture and toss to mix.

Combine the vinegar, oil, onion juice, salt, dry mustard and poppy seeds in a covered jar. Shake to mix well. Pour half the mixture over the salad greens, tossing to coat.

Add the cottage cheese to the remaining vinegar-oil mixture and pour over the salad greens, tossing to coat.

May substitute 1 head iceberg lettuce for the red leaf lettuce. May omit poppy seeds and cottage cheese.

Note: If limiting fat-intake, consider using less bacon or substitute imitation bacon bits.
—*Rebecca Humphrey*

WOODLAND WEDDING SALAD

12 servings

When this salad was served at her daughter's wedding, Sue Pollins had dozens of requests for the recipe. Be sure to serve the salad the day you prepare it, since the cashews tend to get soggy.

1 (16-ounce) package
   frozen baby green peas
1 cup chopped onion
1 cup chopped celery
1/2 cup cauliflowerets
1/2 cup broccoli florets
1/4 cup chopped carrot
1/2 cup raisins

1 cup ranch salad
   dressing
1/2 cup sour cream

1/2 cup toasted cashews

Allow the peas to stand at room temperature until thawed. Drain on paper towels.

Combine the peas, onion, celery, cauliflowerets, broccoli, carrot and raisins in a large bowl.

Combine the salad dressing and sour cream in a small bowl and blend well.

Pour the dressing mixture over the vegetables, tossing to coat.

Chill, covered, for 1 hour.

Sprinkle with the cashews before serving.

If preferred, prepare the salad and allow the unthawed peas to cool the other ingredients, avoiding the chilling time.

May substitute reduced-fat ranch salad dressing for the ranch salad dressing or 1/2 cup plain yogurt for the sour cream. —*Sue Pollins*

BALSAMIC DRESSING

40 servings

Serve over greens or a favorite salad, or use instead of butter on crusty French bread. Be sure to use the specified ingredients for optimum taste.

½ cup virgin olive oil
½ cup roasted garlic
   olive oil
⅓ cup white balsamic
   vinegar
⅓ cup balsamic vinegar
1 rounded teaspoon
   Dijon mustard
1 teaspoon sugar
1 teaspoon
   Worcestershire sauce
Salt to taste
Freshly ground black
   pepper to taste

Combine the olive oils, vinegars, mustard, sugar, Worcestershire sauce, salt and pepper in a large jar and shake well.

Allow the dressing to stand for several hours before serving.

Serve over greens or a favorite salad.

May substitute Italian white wine vinegar for white balsamic vinegar.

Note: The roasted garlic olive oil may be purchased at most gourmet specialty stores.
—*Eve Novak*

CELERY SEED DRESSING

40 servings

A truly delicious homemade dressing, this is an old family recipe.

1 medium yellow onion,
   chopped
¾ cup white vinegar
2 teaspoons salt
2 teaspoons dry mustard
1¼ cups sugar
1½ teaspoons whole
   celery seeds
1 cup canola oil

Combine the onion, vinegar, salt and mustard in a blender container; process until smooth.

Add the sugar gradually, processing until the sugar is completely dissolved. Add the celery seeds and oil, processing until well mixed.

Pour the dressing into a serving container. Serve over greens or a favorite salad.

May substitute cider or herbal vinegar for the white vinegar and vegetable oil for the canola oil.
—*Louise Rahl Bolling*

RASPBERRY VINAIGRETTE DRESSING

54 servings

¼ cup olive oil
¾ cup water
1 cup raspberry vinegar
1 tablespoon chervil
½ tablespoon white
  pepper
1⅓ cups raspberries

Stir the oil, water, vinegar, chervil and white pepper in a medium bowl until blended.

Pour into serving container. Toss with a favorite salad.

May substitute black pepper for white pepper.
—*Summer Friedlander*

ROSE VINEGAR

40 servings

Charlotte has one hundred varieties of Heritage Roses in her extensive gardens and has enjoyed this lovely vinegar for years. Rose hips (the fleshy swollen pod seed capsule of the rose after the petals have fallen off) are a good source of vitamin C and may be included with the petals to make this delicate rose-colored vinegar.

2 cups fragrant rose
  petals
2 cups white vinegar

Pull enough petals to measure about 2 cups. Combine the petals with 2 cups white vinegar in a non-aluminum saucepan. Simmer for 10 minutes.

Strain the vinegar through cheesecloth into a hot sterilized glass container and seal.

Store the vinegar at room temperature and use over fruit. —*Charlotte Bailey*

Preserve the rose-colored tint of Rose Vinegar (which will vary, depending on the color of the rose petals) by using a dark or frosted glass container for storage. In an attractive container, the Rose Vinegar makes a nice and unusual gift.

STEAK AND EGGS BENEDICT

8 servings

Not a dish for those who are watching their weight, this is a great cross between two favorite brunch dishes.

2 egg yolks
1 tablespoon lemon juice
1/4 cup unsalted butter
1 tablespoon horseradish
Dash of white pepper

8 eggs
8 (1-inch thick) beef
　fillets
4 English muffins, split
2 tablespoons butter

Preheat the broiler.

Combine the egg yolks and lemon juice in a blender container; process until smooth.

Heat the butter in a medium saucepan until foamy. Add the hot butter to the egg mixture in a slow stream, processing constantly at high speed until smooth.

Add the horseradish and white pepper; process until smooth.

Pour the mixture into the medium saucepan and warm over low heat; do not allow sauce to boil.

Poach the eggs until the whites are completely set and the yolks just begin to thicken.

Fry the fillets in a cast-iron skillet for 3 minutes on each side or until cooked to taste; drain.

Spread the English muffin halves lightly with the butter. Toast the English muffins.

Layer 1 fillet and 1 egg on each English muffin half on individual serving plates. Spoon the warm sauce over the top and serve immediately.
—*Sheila Quinn Smith*

GRILLED SHRIMP WITH RICE

5 servings

The salsa marinade makes this dish easy, as well as spicy. Serve with a green salad topped with tomato slices, feta cheese and sliced artichoke hearts.

1 pound large shrimp
  with tails, peeled,
  deveined
1 cup salsa

1 cup uncooked rice
1 (4-ounce) jar chopped
  green chiles
1/3 cup chopped scallion
1/2 teaspoon salt
1/2 teaspoon pepper

Mix the shrimp and the salsa in a medium bowl. Chill, covered, for one hour.

Preheat the grill.

Cook the rice according to package directions.

Stir the chiles, scallions, salt and pepper into the rice. Keep warm until ready to serve.

Thread the salsa-coated shrimp onto skewers and grill until cooked through. Do not overcook.

Remove the shrimp from the skewers and serve over the rice. —*Summer Friedlander*

CHILES RELLENOS CASSEROLE

10 servings

This is a very rich and unusual-tasting casserole.

4 (7-ounce) cans mild
  whole green chiles
1 pound Monterey Jack
  cheese, thinly sliced

5 eggs, beaten
1 1/4 cups milk
1/4 cup flour
1/2 teaspoon salt
Dash of pepper
4 cups shredded mild
  Cheddar cheese

Preheat the oven to 350 degrees.

Split the chiles lengthwise; remove the seeds. Drain the chiles. Place the Monterey Jack cheese inside the chiles.

Arrange the stuffed chiles in an ungreased 3-quart baking dish.

Combine the eggs, milk, flour, salt and pepper in a bowl. Beat until smooth. Pour the mixture over the chiles. Sprinkle the Cheddar cheese over the top.

Bake at 350 degrees for 45 minutes or until puffed and golden brown. —*Mae Pierce*

SAVORY MUSHROOM PIE

10 servings

A quiche with a difference—heaven for mushroom lovers.

1/3 cup melted butter
1/4 cup crushed whole
   wheat crackers

1½ pounds fresh
   mushrooms, sliced
4 green onions, sliced
1 clove of garlic, minced
1/4 cup melted butter
2 teaspoons oregano
2 teaspoons basil
1½ teaspoons salt
1½ teaspoons freshly
   ground black pepper
1½ teaspoons chopped
   green bell pepper
1/2 teaspoon thyme
1/2 teaspoon dry mustard
1 teaspoon melted butter

5 eggs, beaten
1 cup half-and-half
Juice and grated rind of
   1/2 lemon

1/2 cup mayonnaise
1/4 cup whipping cream
2 teaspoons chopped
   fresh dill

Mix 1/3 cup butter and cracker crumbs in a small bowl. Press over the bottom of a 9-inch pie plate. Chill until firm.

Preheat the oven to 350 degrees.

Sauté the mushrooms, green onions and garlic in 1/4 cup butter in a medium saucepan until the green onions are tender. Add the oregano, basil, salt, pepper, green pepper, thyme, dry mustard and 1 teaspoon butter; mix well.

Combine the eggs, half-and-half, lemon juice and lemon rind in a bowl.

Stir into the mushroom mixture. Pour into the chilled pie shell. Bake at 350 degrees for 25 minutes.

Blend the mayonnaise, whipping cream and dill in a small bowl. Spread the mayonnaise mixture over the top of the pie sealing to the edge.

Bake for 20 to 25 minutes longer or until a knife inserted near the center comes out clean. Serve hot. —*Marge Lentz*

REAL MAN'S QUICHE

4 servings

Serve this recipe with fresh fruit for Sunday brunch by the pool. Real men—and women—will love it.

4 ounces Jarlsburg
  cheese, shredded
1 tablespoon flour
1/4 cup sliced green
  onions
1 teaspoon of dried
  parsley
Pinch of nutmeg
Salt and pepper to taste
1 unbaked (9-inch) pie
  shell

4 eggs, beaten
1 1/2 cups half-and-half
5 slices bacon, partially
  cooked, cut into pieces
5 sausage links, cooked,
  drained

Preheat the oven to 375 degrees.

Toss the cheese with the flour in a small bowl. Stir in the green onions, parsley, nutmeg, salt and pepper. Sprinkle into the pie shell.

Whisk the eggs with the half-and-half and pour over the cheese mixture.

Bake at 375 degrees for 35 minutes. Remove from the oven.

Arrange the bacon and sausage decoratively on top. Bake for 10 minutes longer or until a knife inserted near the center comes out clean.

Serve hot.

May substitute Swiss cheese for Jarlsburg, use egg substitute for eggs, substitute skim milk for the half-and-half, or omit or reduce the amounts of the bacon and sausage. —*Mary Ann McGuigan*

Reduce the baking time of quiches by partially prebaking the pie shell. Always prick the bottom and side of the shell to prevent puffing.

HERBED CHEESE STRUDEL

8 servings

Although the phyllo dough must be thawed and the ricotta cheese must be drained for eight to twelve hours, this delicious strudel is well worth the time involved.

2 cups ricotta cheese
4 sheets frozen phyllo
   dough

1 clove of garlic
1/2 teaspoon salt
2 egg yolks
1/2 teaspoon dried thyme
1/2 teaspoon dried savory
1/2 teaspoon dried
   tarragon
4 tablespoons chopped
   chives
1 1/2 teaspoons chopped
   fresh parsley

1/2 to 3/4 cup bread
   crumbs
1 1/2 teaspoons melted
   butter
1 cup melted unsalted
   butter
2 egg whites

Drain the ricotta cheese in a mesh strainer over a small bowl for several hours. Thaw the phyllo dough in the refrigerator for 8 to 12 hours.

Preheat the oven to 375 degrees.

Spoon the drained ricotta cheese into a medium bowl.

Press the unpeeled garlic through a garlic press, using a knife to scrape off the garlic as it is pressed through the holes.

Combine the pressed garlic, salt, egg yolks, thyme, savory, tarragon, chives and parsley with the ricotta cheese. Set aside.

Brown the bread crumbs in the 1 1/2 teaspoons butter in a small skillet over low heat.

Place 1 sheet of the phyllo dough on a nonporous work surface. Brush with the unsalted butter. Layer another sheet on top, brushing with the unsalted butter and dusting with a sprinkling of bread crumbs. Repeat the process with the remaining phyllo.

Beat the egg whites in a mixer bowl until stiff peaks form. Fold into the cheese mixture. Spread the mixture 2 inches wide on one long end of the dough, leaving a border on all sides.

Roll as for a jelly roll, sealing the edge and ends and brushing with unsalted butter at each turn. Place seam side down on a buttered baking sheet. Brush the top and sides of the roll with unsalted butter. Sprinkle lightly with bread crumbs. Bake at 375 degrees for 25 to 30 minutes.

Remove the strudel from the baking sheet onto a serving platter. Slice and serve immediately.
—Linda Austin

CRANBERRY COFFEE CAKE

15 servings

This recipe, passed down from Claudia's grandmother, is especially good during the holiday season.

1 cup margarine, softened
1 cup sugar
2 eggs

2 cups flour
1 tablespoon baking powder
1/2 teaspoon salt
1 cup sour cream
1/2 teaspoon almond extract

1 (16-ounce) can whole cranberry sauce
1/2 cup slivered almonds

1 cup confectioners' sugar
1 tablespoon milk
1/2 teaspoon vanilla extract

Preheat the oven to 350 degrees.

Cream the margarine in a large mixer bowl. Add the sugar gradually, beating well after each addition until light and fluffy. Add the eggs 1 at a time, mixing well after each addition.

Sift the flour, baking powder and salt together. Add to the creamed mixture alternately with the sour cream, mixing well after each addition. Stir in the almond flavoring.

Pour the batter into a greased and floured 9x13-inch cake pan.

Spread the cranberry sauce lightly over the batter. Sprinkle the almonds over the top.

Bake at 350 degrees for 35 to 40 minutes.

Combine the confectioners' sugar, milk and vanilla in a small bowl; mix well.

Drizzle the glaze over the hot cake.

May substitute 2 cups self-rising flour for the all-purpose flour, omitting the baking powder and salt. —*Claudia Harbaugh*

CARROT BREAD

24 servings

1 (8-ounce) can crushed
   pineapple
3 cups flour
2 teaspoons baking soda
1/2 teaspoon baking
   powder
1 1/2 teaspoons cinnamon

3/4 cup vegetable oil
2 cups sugar
2 teaspoons vanilla
   extract
3 eggs
2 cups shredded carrots
3/4 cup chopped walnuts

Preheat the oven to 350 degrees.

Drain the pineapple, reserving 1 tablespoon of the juice.

Combine the flour, baking soda, baking powder and cinnamon in a small bowl; mix well.

Beat the oil, sugar and vanilla in a mixer bowl. Add the eggs 1 at a time and mix well after each addition.

Stir the pineapple, carrots and reserved pineapple juice into the sugar mixture.

Add the dry ingredients; stir just until moistened. Stir in the walnuts.

Spoon the batter into 2 greased 5x9-inch loaf pans.

Bake at 350 degrees for 1 hour or until a wooden pick inserted in the center comes out clean. Cool in the pans for 10 minutes. Remove the loaves to a wire rack to cool completely. Serve with cream cheese.

May omit the carrots and pineapple juice and use 2 cups shredded zucchini. —*Tracy Morford*

BLUEBERRY BLISS MUFFINS

18 muffins

An absolute blueberry lover's delight! Even those non-blueberry lovers may end up asking for seconds.

1/2 cup butter or margarine, softened
1 cup sugar
2 eggs
2 cups flour
2 teaspoons baking powder
1/2 teaspoon salt
1/2 cup milk
1 teaspoon vanilla extract
2 1/2 cups blueberries

Preheat the oven to 375 degrees.

Cream the butter and sugar in a mixer bowl until light and fluffy.

Add the eggs 1 at a time, mixing well after each addition.

Mix the flour, baking powder and salt together. Add to the creamed mixture alternately with the milk and vanilla, mixing well after each addition.

Crush 1/2 cup of the blueberries and stir into the batter. Fold in the remaining 2 cups blueberries.

Fill 18 greased muffin cups 3/4 full. Sprinkle with additional sugar.

Bake at 375 degrees for 30 minutes or until a wooden pick inserted in the center comes out clean. Cool in the pans for 5 minutes; remove to a wire rack to cool completely.

May use miniature muffin cups to make 2 to 3 dozen bite-size muffins. —*Lisa R. Moeller*

For a terrific dessert, bake the muffin batter in a greased 8x8-inch baking pan and cut into squares; then top with ice cream and more blueberries.

RASPBERRY STREUSEL MUFFINS

12 muffins

The streusel that tops these dense hearty muffins says, "Taste me!"

2 cups flour
1/2 teaspoon baking powder
1/2 teaspoon baking soda
1/2 teaspoon cinnamon
1/4 teaspoon salt

1/2 cup milk
1/2 cup sour cream
1 teaspoon vanilla extract

1/2 cup sugar
1/2 cup butter, softened
1 egg
1 cup fresh raspberries

1/2 cup flour
1/2 cup quick-cooking oats
1/3 cup sugar
1/2 teaspoon cinnamon
1/2 teaspoon salt
6 tablespoons butter
2 to 4 tablespoons confectioners' sugar

Preheat the oven to 400 degrees.

Grease 12 oversize or 16 regular size muffin cups.

Mix the flour, baking powder, baking soda, cinnamon and salt in a medium bowl and set aside. Beat the milk with the sour cream and vanilla in a small bowl until smooth and set aside.

Cream the sugar and butter in a large mixer bowl, beating until light and fluffy. Add the egg and beat until well blended.

Add the flour mixture and the sour cream mixture to the creamed mixture alternately, mixing just until moistened after each addition.

Fold in the raspberries gently and spoon into the prepared muffin cups, filling each cup 2/3 full.

Combine the flour, oats, sugar, cinnamon and salt in a medium bowl; mix well. Cut in the butter until crumbly. Sprinkle over the batter.

Bake at 400 degrees for 20 to 25 minutes or until golden brown. Remove from the muffin cups.

Sprinkle the cooled muffins with confectioners' sugar.

May use light sour cream if preferred. May substitute blueberries for the raspberries.
—*Carol Vallozzi*

ZUCCHINI AND BASIL MUFFINS

22 muffins

1 cup vegetable oil
¾ cup sugar
3 eggs

2 cups flour
2 teaspoons baking
  powder
½ teaspoon salt
¼ teaspoon freshly
  ground black pepper
¼ teaspoon grated
  nutmeg

1 cup grated unpeeled
  zucchini
½ cup chopped fresh
  basil leaves
½ teaspoon grated
  lemon rind

Preheat the oven to 350 degrees. Grease muffin pans lightly.

Combine the oil and sugar in a mixer bowl; beat well. Add the eggs 1 at a time, mixing well after each addition.

Sift the flour, baking powder, salt, pepper and nutmeg together. Add to the sugar mixture; stir just until moistened.

Fold in the zucchini, basil leaves and lemon rind.

Spoon into the lightly greased muffin cups, filling each cup ⅔ full.

Bake at 350 degrees for 25 to 35 minutes or until a wooden pick inserted in the center of a muffin comes out clean.

Cool in the pans on wire racks for 10 minutes; remove the muffins to wire racks to cool completely. —*Carol Vallozzi*

EASY COLD-OVEN POPOVERS

12 muffins or 6 popovers

These easy, buttery popovers go well with soups, salads or any main dish. Bake in muffin cups for small popovers or, if you have a popover pan or custard cups, make just six big, crusty popovers.

2 eggs, at room
    temperature
1/4 teaspoon salt
1 cup milk
2 tablespoons melted
    unsalted butter
1 cup flour

Whisk the eggs and salt lightly in a medium bowl.

Add the milk, butter and flour, mixing just until blended.

Spoon the mixture into buttered muffin cups, filling each cup 1/2 full.

Place in a cold oven. Heat the oven to 425 degrees. Bake for 20 minutes.

Reduce the oven temperature to 375 degrees. Bake for 10 to 15 minutes longer or until the popovers are golden brown and crisp on top.

Turn off the oven. Pierce each popover with a skewer to release steam. Let the popovers stand in the closed oven for 2 to 3 minutes longer.

Serve immediately with butter. —*Eve Novak*

FRENCH TOAST A LA ORANGE

8 servings

Baking French toast makes serving a crowd easy.

1/4 cup melted butter
1/3 cup sugar
1/2 teaspoon cinnamon
1 teaspoon fresh orange zest

4 eggs, beaten
2/3 cup orange juice
1 teaspoon vanilla extract
8 thick slices white bread
2 to 3 tablespoons confectioners' sugar

Preheat the oven to 325 degrees.

Pour the butter into a 10x15-inch baking pan. Sprinkle with the sugar, cinnamon and orange zest.

Whisk the eggs lightly with the orange juice and vanilla in a small bowl. Dip the bread slices in the egg mixture, coating both sides. Arrange the bread slices in the prepared pan.

Bake at 325 degrees for 20 minutes or until golden brown.

Remove the French toast from the pan with a spatula and cut each slice into 2 triangles. Arrange triangles on a serving platter and sprinkle with confectioners' sugar. —*Joan Beidler*

Prepare up to the baking point the night before and chill, covered, overnight. Serve with syrup or a light orange sauce or simply garnish with strawberries, melon or favorite fruit.

VERY LIGHT AND EXCELLENT WAFFLES

5 waffles

These waffles are light and very tasty. Try serving with blueberry sauce (see page 159), strawberries or other favorite fresh fruits.

1³/₄ cups sifted flour
3 teaspoons baking
    powder
3 egg yolks, beaten
1¹/₄ cups 2% milk
¹/₂ cup vegetable oil
3 to 4 egg whites

Preheat the waffle iron.

Sift the flour and baking powder into a medium bowl.

Combine the egg yolks and milk and stir into the flour mixture. Add the oil and mix well.

Beat the egg whites in a small mixer bowl until stiff peaks form. Fold the egg whites into the batter.

Pour the batter onto the waffle iron and bake using the manufacturer's instructions. —*Dick Morford*

Replace the liquid in your pancake recipe with club soda for the lightest pancakes ever. This batter must be used at once, however, as the soda goes flat.

CELEBRATION BREAD PUDDING

16 servings

A rich, fruity dessert, this bread pudding also make a good brunch dish.

1/2 cup (scant) raisins
1 cup boiling water
10 eggs
2¼ cups sugar
4 cups milk
1 tablespoon vanilla
  extract

14 slices dried white
  bread, crusts
  trimmed, cubed
1 cup melted butter
2 large Golden Delicious
  apples, chopped

Cinnamon, nutmeg or
  confectioners' sugar

Plump the raisins in boiling water to cover for 10 minutes. Drain and set aside.

Preheat the oven to 350 degrees.

Combine the eggs and sugar in a large mixer bowl. Beat at medium speed until the sugar is dissolved.

Bring the milk and vanilla just to the boiling point in a large saucepan over medium heat.

Add the hot milk mixtute in a slow stream to the egg mixture, stirring constantly.

Layer half the bread cubes in a 10x15-inch stainless steel baking pan. Drizzle half the melted butter over the bread. Add layers of raisins, apples and the remaining bread cubes. Drizzle the remaining butter over the bread. Pour the milk and egg mixture evenly over the top.

Bake at 350 degrees for 45 to 60 minutes or until golden brown.

Serve hot or warm.

Garnish with cinnamon, confectioners' sugar or nutmeg at serving time. —*Win Beidler*

EN PLEIN AIR

Led by the French Impressionists at the end of the 19th century, American artists began to take their canvasses and palettes into forest and field to paint. There they worked from nature's true inspiration rather than remembrances conjured up in the dim confines of their studios. This school was known as the "plein air" style, meaning "in the open air." Artists' summer colonies sprang up in Old Lyme, Connecticut, and East Hampton, New York. In southwestern Pennsylvania, George Hetzel, with fellow artists and students, continued this tradition at Scalp Level near Johnstown. The Westmoreland Museum of Art has an important collection of landscapes by Hetzel and his followers.

To enjoy the hours out-of-doors, the artists frequently carried along, in addition to their painting supplies, full picnic hampers of food packed for the day.

Robert Henri (1865-1929)
Picnic at Meshoppen, Pennsylvania, July 4, 1902
Oil on Canvas, 26 x 32 inches
Gift of William A. Coulter Fund

ZESTY HUMMUS DIP

10 servings

Slices of red, yellow or green bell peppers are delicious for dipping and make an attractive arrangement around the bowl of dip.

2 (8-ounce) cans
   chick-peas
Juice of 2 lemons
1 tablespoon olive oil
1 clove of garlic, chopped
1/2 cup tahini
1 tablespoon chopped
   parsley
1/2 teaspoon cumin
1/8 teaspoon cayenne
1/8 teaspoon paprika
1 tablespoon chopped
   parsley

Drain the chick-peas, reserving 1 tablespoon of the liquid.

Combine the chick-peas, reserved liquid, lemon juice, olive oil and garlic in a food processor container. Process until smooth. Add the tahini, 1 tablespoon parsley, cumin and cayenne. Process until blended.

Spoon into a serving bowl and sprinkle with paprika. Top with the remaining parsley.

Serve with pita chips or pita wedges.
—*Audrey Stern*

FRUITED MINT TEA

8 servings

A combination of mint and fruit flavors make this a very refreshing thirst quencher.

3 cups boiling water
4 tea bags
12 fresh mint leaves

1 cup sugar
1/4 cup fresh lemon juice
1 cup orange juice
5 cups cold water

Pour the boiling water over the tea bags and mint leaves in a pitcher.

Cover and steep for 5 minutes. Remove the tea bags and mint, squeezing gently.

Stir in the sugar, lemon juice, orange juice and cold water.

Serve in tall glasses over crushed ice. Garnish with sprigs of mint. —*Marilyn Gaut*

BLOODY MARY MIX

6 servings

Garnish drinks with celery sticks with a few leaves attached.

1 (32-ounce) can tomato
   juice
1/2 teaspoon
   Worcestershire sauce
1/2 teaspoon Tabasco
   sauce
1/2 teaspoon seasoned
   salt
Celery seeds to taste
Freshly ground pepper
   to taste
Vodka to taste
6 wedges of fresh lime

Pour the tomato juice into a large pitcher and add the Worcestershire sauce, Tabasco sauce, seasoned salt, celery seeds and pepper. Stir until well mixed. Chill for 12 hours.

Combine 6 ounces of the mix with a generous shot of vodka for each serving. Serve over ice in lime-rimmed glasses. —*The Women's Committee*

CORN AND CHICKEN SOUP

4 servings

Bud Gibbons, a well-known local artist, frequently paints out-of-doors and takes this hearty soup along in a thermos as the weather turns cool.

2 whole chicken breasts,
   skinned and boned
1/4 cup vegetable oil
2 small onions, coarsely
   chopped
1 cup chicken broth
2 carrots, thinly sliced
2 stalks celery, thinly
   sliced
2 (10-ounce) cans
   cream-style golden
   corn soup
Salt to taste
1 teaspoon freshly
   ground pepper

Rinse the chicken and pat dry; cut into bite-size pieces. Heat the oil in a wok. Add the chicken. Stir-fry over high heat until tender.

Push the chicken to the side of the wok. Add the onions. Stir-fry just until the onions are tender. Add 1/2 cup of the chicken broth. Add the carrots, celery and corn soup; mix with the chicken.

Season with salt and pepper. Pour in the remaining 1/2 cup chicken broth. Simmer, loosely covered, until some of the liquid is absorbed and the chicken and vegetables are tender.

Ladle into soup bowls. Garnish with parsley and chives. Serve with warm crusty bread.
—*Bud Gibbons*

COLD CUCUMBER SOUP

8 servings

Ideal for summer entertaining, this soup is extremely easy to prepare and perfect for creative garnishing.

5 large cucumbers
Salt to taste

½ cup chopped parsley
6 scallions, chopped
2 tablespoons freshly chopped dill
¼ cup lemon juice
1 quart buttermilk
2 cups sour cream
Freshly ground white pepper to taste

Finely sliced radishes
Finely cubed cucumber
Fresh mint leaves
Tiny, fresh poached shrimp
Finely minced lobster meat

Peel the cucumbers and slice into halves lengthwise, discarding the seeds.

Place the cucumbers in a bowl and sprinkle with salt. Let stand for 30 minutes; drain.

Chop the cucumbers coarsely and combine with the parsley, scallions, dill, lemon juice, buttermilk and sour cream in a blender or food processor container. Process at high speed until smooth.

Add salt and white pepper. Chill until serving time. Pour into a large tureen.

Garnish with radishes, cucumbers, mint leaves, shrimp or lobster meat. —*Andee Millstein*

When we eat, we experience an indefinable and peculiar sensation of well-being, arising out of our inner consciousness; so that by the mere act of eating we repair our losses, and add to the number of our years.
—Fernand Point (1897–1955) Restaurateur

Spicy Gazpacho

6 servings

Try serving this chunky "salad-in-a-soup bowl" as a salsa with chips or as a zesty sauce with poultry or seafood. Reduce the vegetable juice cocktail to adjust the consistency.

3 large tomatoes
1 cucumber
1/2 cup finely chopped
   green bell pepper
1/2 cup finely chopped
   yellow bell pepper
3 jalapeños, diced
2 tablespoons chopped
   onion
2 tablespoons chopped
   scallion

3 cups vegetable juice
   cocktail
1 tablespoon fresh
   chopped parsley
1 tablespoon finely
   chopped cilantro
1/2 teaspoon red pepper
1/2 teaspoon cayenne
1/2 teaspoon cumin
1/3 teaspoon white pepper
1 teaspoon Tabasco
   sauce

Cucumber slices
Chopped fresh cilantro
Chopped fresh parsley

Peel, seed and finely chop the tomatoes and cucumber. Combine with the bell peppers, jalapeños, onion and scallion in a large bowl; mix well.

Add the vegetable juice, parsley, cilantro, red pepper, cayenne, cumin, white pepper and Tabasco sauce.

May purée the gazpacho in a blender or food processor for 12 seconds for a smoother texture.

Chill for 2 hours or longer. Pour into soup plates.

Garnish with cucumber slices, fresh chopped cilantro or parsley. —*Summer Friedlander*

The best cooking is that which takes into consideration the products of the season.

BOK CHOY SALAD

12 servings

Easy to prepare and a nice alternative to tossed green salads.

2 packages ramen
    noodles
1/2 cup sliced almonds
5 green onions, thinly
    sliced
4 tablespoons margarine
1 head bok choy
1/4 cup sesame seeds

1 cup vegetable oil
1/2 cup vinegar
1 tablespoon soy sauce
1/2 cup sugar

Crush the noodles and discard the seasoning packet or reserve for another purpose.

Sauté the noodles, almonds and green onions in the margarine in a saucepan until the noodles are golden brown. Let stand until cool.

Slice the bok choy very finely.

Combine the noodle mixture with the bok choy and sesame seeds in a bowl; toss gently. Chill until serving time.

Combine the oil, vinegar, soy sauce and sugar in a small bowl and mix well.

Add the dressing to the salad; toss to coat well.
—*Elizabeth C. Rodgers*

Serve "summer in a bowl" with a panzanella salad by combining chunks of fresh tomatoes and Italian bread, red onions, black olives and a vinaigrette of olive oil, red wine vinegar and fresh basil.

BLACK BEAN SALAD

4 servings

Margot Birmingham Perot is proud to claim Greensburg as her hometown. She grew up here, graduated from high school, and she and Ross were married in the First Presbyterian Church on Main Street. A family favorite of Ross and Margot Perot, this unusual, high-protein salad could become a favorite at your house, too.

1 (20-ounce) can black beans
1 (8-ounce) can whole kernel corn
1 large tomato, chopped
2 tablespoons olive oil
Juice of 1 lime
1 tablespoon cumin
½ bunch cilantro, chopped
1 pickled jalapeño, chopped
2 cloves of garlic, minced
Salt and pepper to taste

Drain the black beans and corn. Rinse under cold running water and drain well.

Combine the beans and corn in a large bowl, tossing to mix.

Stir in the tomato, olive oil, lime juice and cumin; mix gently.

Add the cilantro, jalapeño, garlic, salt and pepper; mix well.

Chill for 8 hours or longer.
—*Ross and Margot Perot*

Great cuisine is intuitive. A solid base in the fundamentals is vital, but ultimately it is the senses—smell, taste, sight, feel—that tell the cuisinier when a dish is great and not merely adequate.
—Fernand Point (1897–1955), Restaurateur

Couscous and Sun-Dried Tomatoes

8 servings

Prepare this recipe a day ahead, refrigerate overnight and allow it to come to room temperature before serving. It is delightful with almost any meal but outstanding as a luncheon salad.

2 cups chicken broth
3 whole sun-dried
   tomatoes, julienned
1 tablespoon olive oil
1 cup uncooked couscous

1 tablespoon olive oil
1 small onion, chopped
1 clove of garlic, minced

1/2 teaspoon rosemary
1/2 teaspoon chopped
   fresh parsley
1/2 teaspoon thyme
3 tablespoons orange
   juice
1 teaspoon grated
   orange zest
Salt and pepper to taste
1 to 2 tablespoons olive
   oil

Sliced black olives
Walnuts

Combine the chicken broth, tomatoes and 1 tablespoon olive oil in a saucepan.

Bring to a boil over high heat and stir in the couscous. Remove from heat and let stand, covered, for 5 minutes.

Heat 1 tablespoon olive oil in a small skillet and add the onion and garlic. Cook until tender.

Add the onion garlic mixture to the couscous mixture.

Stir in the rosemary, parsley, thyme, orange juice, orange zest, salt and pepper.

Cool to room temperature. Add 1 to 2 tablespoons olive oil. Spoon into a serving bowl. Garnish with sliced black olives and walnuts.

To serve as a hot side dish, omit the last 1 to 2 tablespoons olive oil. —*Vernie West*

FRENCH RIVER CUCUMBER SALAD

4 servings

A favorite family recipe from summer holidays on the French River, this salad is the perfect accompaniment for grilled or barbecued entrées.

1 unpeeled large
  cucumber, thinly
  sliced
1 medium sweet onion,
  thinly sliced
Salt
½ cup sour cream
Paprika to taste

Place the cucumber and onions in separate dishes. Sprinkle the cucumbers with salt and add enough water to cover. Sprinkle the onion with salt. Chill both, covered, for 8 to 10 hours.

Drain the cucumber and onions. Combine with the sour cream in a bowl; mix gently. Sprinkle with paprika. Chill, covered, until serving time

Serve with grilled fish on a bed of spinach for a great luncheon dish. May substitute 4 to 6 sliced green onions for the sweet onion.
—*Charlotte B. Bailey*

GREEN BEANS SEBASTIAN

4 servings

A seasonal dish appropriate for picnics and summer parties, the green beans may be served with a platter of sliced ham and potato salad.

2 pounds fresh green
  beans
½ cup virgin olive oil
10 cloves of garlic,
  chopped
¼ teaspoon salt
¼ teaspoon white pepper

Wash the green beans, snapping off only the ends of the beans and leaving the beans whole.

Blanch the beans in a generous amount of boiling water in a 6-quart saucepan for 4 or 5 minutes or until tender-crisp. Refresh with cold water to stop the cooking and to retain the color and crispness.

Combine the olive oil, garlic, salt and white pepper in a porcelain bowl. Add the beans; toss to coat well. Chill, covered, until serving time.
—*Dr. Paul A. Chew*

RED POTATO SALAD WITH GRILLED SCALLIONS

6 servings

1½ pounds small red
  potatoes
2 tablespoons chopped
  green bell pepper
2 tablespoons chopped
  red bell pepper
2 tablespoons chopped
  yellow bell pepper
2 tablespoons diagonally
  sliced scallion

½ cup low-calorie
  mayonnaise
6 tablespoons vinegar
1 clove of garlic,
  crushed, finely
  chopped
2 tablespoons chopped
  onion
1 tablespoon basil
1 teaspoon oregano
1 teaspoon celery seeds
1 teaspoon dry mustard
2 teaspoons chopped
  cilantro
2 teaspoons dill

12 scallions

Cut the unpeeled potatoes into quarters. Cook in water to cover in a saucepan just until tender; drain. Set the potatoes aside to cool.

Combine the potatoes with the green, red and yellow bell peppers and sliced scallion in a bowl.

Blend the mayonnaise and vinegar in a bowl. Stir in the garlic, onion, basil, oregano, celery seeds, dry mustard, cilantro and dill. Pour over the vegetable mixture, tossing until coated.

Chill until serving time.

Trim the 12 scallions into 6-inch lengths. Grill lightly over hot coals.

Serve the potato salad on lettuce-lined salad plates. Top with the grilled scallions.
—*Summer Friedlander*

QUINOA SALAD

8 servings

Quinoa (pronounced "keen-wa"), an ancient grain from South America, contains more high-quality protein than any other grain.

5 cups quinoa
1 cup chopped carrots
3/4 cup minced parsley
1 cup sunflower seeds
4 cloves of garlic,
   chopped

1/4 cup olive oil
1/4 cup soy sauce
1/2 cup lemon juice

Cook the quinoa according to package instructions. Set aside to cool.

Combine the quinoa with the carrot, parsley, sunflower seeds and garlic in a large serving bowl.

Mix the olive oil, soy sauce and lemon juice in a small bowl. Add to the quinoa mixture; toss lightly. Chill until serving time. Garnish with tomato wedges and serve on lettuce.
—Sue Birmingham

FLANK STEAK NOVA SCOTIA

4 servings

This is a favorite family recipe from summer holidays spent in Nova Scotia. The marinade is a little different and can be used as a sauce.

1 cup catsup
1/2 cup water
1 tablespoon paprika
1 tablespoon sugar
1 clove of garlic, minced
1 medium onion, finely
   chopped
1/3 cup vinegar
1 tablespoon
   Worcestershire sauce
1/4 cup butter

1 (1-pound) flank steak

Combine the catsup, water, paprika, sugar, garlic and onion in a saucepan. Bring to a boil; reduce the heat. Simmer for 10 minutes. Remove from the heat and add the vinegar, Worcestershire sauce and butter. Cool to room temperature.

Place the flank steak in a dish and pour the sauce over it, coating completely. Marinate for 8 to 24 hours, covered, in the refrigerator. Drain, reserving the marinade.

Preheat the grill over hot coals.

Prick the steak with a fork on all sides. Grill the steak for 3 to 6 minutes per side for rare or until done to taste.

Cut the steak almost horizontally into 1/2-inch to 1-inch slices to serve. Heat the reserved marinade and serve as a sauce. —Vernie S. West

GRILLED LEG OF LAMB

8 servings

Try this very special recipe for a special occasion or a more formal outdoor affair as a nice change from steak. Wild rice and grilled mushrooms are good accompaniments. Use whatever fresh herbs your garden offers—fennel, mint, parsley, rosemary or others in season. Grilled onions are conveniently prepared over the hot coals at the same time as the lamb.

Classic Vinaigrette
  (see below)
1 (4-pound) leg of lamb,
  butterflied
1 tablespoon whole
  black peppercorns,
  cracked
2 bunches fresh herbs
3 sweet onions, cut into
  halves (optional)

Mint jelly
Sprigs of fresh mint

Pour the Classic Vinaigrette into a shallow dish. Add the lamb and cracked peppercorns.

Marinate in the refrigerator for 4 hours or longer, turning several times; drain.

Preheat the grill.

Spread half of the fresh herbs over a steel double-sided grill rack. Add the lamb and onions; top with the remaining herbs.

Grill for 8 to 10 minutes on each side or until done to taste.

Place the lamb on a platter. Serve with the grilled onions and mint jelly. Garnish with fresh sprigs of mint.

CLASSIC VINAIGRETTE

3/4 cup

1/4 cup red wine vinegar
3/4 cup olive oil
1/2 teaspoon Dijon
  mustard
1/2 teaspoon salt
1/8 teaspoon freshly
  ground pepper

Combine the wine vinegar, olive oil, mustard, salt and pepper in a jar; shake until well mixed.
—*Jill Cook*

GRILLED BREAST OF CHICKEN

4 servings

This savory chicken is also delicious sliced and served as a salad on a bed of lettuce with a vinaigrette dressing. Serve hot off the grill with a green vegetable, a rice or potato dish and a crisp salad.

2 whole chicken breasts,
  split, skinned, boned
Juice of 1 lemon
1 teaspoon dried oregano
1 teaspoon dried thyme
1 teaspoon dried savory
Pinch of rosemary,
  crushed
1/4 teaspoon marjoram
Freshly ground pepper
  to taste
1 teaspoon paprika
1 1/2 teaspoons olive oil

Rinse the chicken and pat dry; place on a plate.

Sprinkle with the lemon juice. Season with a mixture of the oregano, thyme, savory, rosemary, marjoram, pepper and paprika. Drizzle with the olive oil. Let stand for 15 minutes.

Preheat the grill or the broiler.

Grill the chicken for 20 minutes or until firm to touch, turning 1 or more times. —*Linda Austin*

Poultry is for the cook what canvas is to the painter. It is served to us boiled, roasted, fried, hot or cold, whole or in pieces, with or without sauce, boned, skinned, stuffed, and always with equal success.
—Brillat-Savarin, 19th Century French gastronome

TOMATO CHEESE TART

8 servings

A satisfying main dish or a delicious side dish with grilled fish, serve this tart as an expecially satisfying main dish when fresh garden tomatoes are available.

1½ cups flour
1 teaspoon salt
6 tablespoons shortening
¼ cup orange juice

3 tablespoons Dijon
  mustard
2 cups mixed shredded
  mozzarella and
  Cheddar cheese
5 medium ripe tomatoes,
  thinly sliced
Salt and pepper to taste
2 cloves of garlic, finely
  chopped
1 tablespoon olive oil
1 teaspoon dried basil
1 tablespoon Parmesan
  cheese

Combine the flour and salt in a medium bowl and mix well. Cut in the shortening. Stir in the orange juice with a fork until mixture forms a dough.

Shape the dough into a ball and place on a piece of waxed paper. Top with another sheet of waxed paper and roll into an 11-inch circle. Chill while preparing filling.

Preheat the oven to 400 degrees.

Fit the pastry into a 10-inch pie plate, fluting the edge. Spread the mustard on the bottom of the pastry. Sprinkle with the cheese mixture.

Arrange the tomato slices in overlapping concentric circles over the cheese. Sprinkle with salt and pepper. Drizzle with olive oil and sprinkle with the garlic, basil and Parmesan cheese.

Bake at 400 degrees for 35 to 40 minutes or until bubbly in the center.

Cool for 15 minutes before slicing.

Garnish with additional fresh basil leaves.
—*Karen Rich Douglas*

LEMON POPPY SEED POUND CAKE

12 servings

This is a favorite for Christmas gift-giving. It has a light texture and a subtle flavor.

1/2 cup butter
3 eggs
1/2 cup lemon yogurt
1 1/2 cups flour
1/4 teaspoon baking powder
1/8 teaspoon baking soda
1 cup sugar
1/2 teaspoon vanilla extract
2 tablespoons lemon juice
1 teaspoon grated lemon zest
2 tablespoons poppy seeds

Preheat the oven to 325 degrees.

Let the butter, eggs and yogurt stand at room temperature.

Mix the flour, baking powder and baking soda and set aside.

Cream the butter in a mixer bowl until creamy. Add the sugar 2 tablespoons at a time, beating at medium-high speed after each addition until light and fluffy. Add the vanilla, lemon juice and lemon zest; mix well. Add the eggs 1 at a time, beating at medium-low speed for 1 minute after each addition or until smooth.

Add the flour mixture alternately with the yogurt, mixing at low speed until just combined.

Fold in the poppy seeds. Spoon into a greased and floured 5x9-inch loaf pan.

Bake at 325 degrees for 55 to 60 minutes or until the cake tests done. Cool in the pan on a wire rack for 10 minutes. Invert onto a cake plate. Let stand until cooled completely.

Garnish with a sifting of confectioners' sugar.
—Sarah Henry

CHOCOLATE LOVER'S PECAN BROWNIES

16 brownies

3/4 cup sugar
1/3 cup butter
2 tablespoons water
1 cup semisweet
    chocolate chips
1 teaspoon vanilla extract

2 eggs
1/4 cup flour
1/4 teaspoon baking soda
1 cup semisweet
    chocolate chips
1/2 cup chopped pecans
    or cashews

Preheat the oven to 325 degrees.

Combine the sugar, butter and water in a small saucepan. Bring to a boil over medium heat, stirring constantly. Remove from the heat and stir in 1 cup chocolate chips and the vanilla. Stir until the chocolate chips are melted and the mixture is smooth.

Pour into a medium bowl to cool. Add the eggs 1 at a time, beating well after each addition. Add a mixture of the flour and baking soda; mix well.

Stir in the remaining 1 cup chocolate chips and pecans until well mixed. Pour into a greased and floured 9x9-inch baking pan. Bake at 325 degrees for 30 minutes or until the brownies pull from the sides of the pan. Cool in the pan on a wire rack. Cut into squares and serve with vanilla ice cream.
—*Isabel Haggerson*

POTATO CHIP COOKIES

24 cookies

1 cup butter or
    margarine, softened
1/2 cup sugar
1 1/2 cups flour
1 cup finely ground
    cashews
1 cup crushed potato
    chips
1/4 cup (or more)
    confectioners' sugar

Preheat the oven to 325 degrees.

Cream the butter and sugar in a medium mixer bowl until light and fluffy. Add the flour and cashews. Chill for 1 to 2 hours. Add the potato chips; mix well.

Shape into 1-inch balls and place on a greased cookie sheet. Press with a fork in a crisscross design.

Bake at 325 degrees for 12 to 15 minutes or until golden brown. Remove to brown paper. Let stand until cool. Sprinkle both sides with confectioners' sugar. —*Alice McKenna*

LUSCIOUS LINZER TART

6 to 8 servings

A wonderful dessert to serve at a small dinner party.

1 cup finely slivered
  almonds

2 cups flour
1 cup sugar
1 teaspoon cinnamon
1/4 teaspoon ground
  cloves
3/4 cup butter

1 egg
1 tablespoon kirsch
1 (10- to 12-ounce) jar
  raspberry preserves

Preheat the oven to 350 degrees.

Spread the almonds in a single layer on a baking sheet. Toast at 350 degrees for 10 minutes or just until lightly browned. Process the toasted almonds in a food processor until finely ground.

Mix the flour, sugar, cinnamon, cloves and almonds in a medium bowl; process with the butter in a food processor until crumbly.

Beat the egg and kirsch in a small bowl until blended. Place the flour mixture in a large bowl, making a well in the center of the mixture. Spoon the egg mixture into the well and mix with a fork to form a dough. Reserve 1/3 of the dough.

Press the remaining dough into a 9-inch tart pan with a removable bottom. Spread the raspberry preserves in the prepared pan.

Roll out the reserved dough on a floured surface. Cut into 1-inch strips with a pastry cutter. Arrange the strips in a lattice pattern over the raspberry preserves.

Bake at 350 degrees for 40 to 45 minutes or until golden brown. Cool completely on a wire rack before removing the side of the pan.
—Joan DeRose

To make a more decorative edge on the lattice strip, use a scalloped-edge cutter when cutting the pastry.

THE CURATOR'S ROLE

A museum curator is like a good chef when putting together an exhibition. First, the idea for the exhibition must be conceived, and then the objects to be presented must be collected. Style, color, texture, media, and size are all elements to be taken into consideration during the research and planning. The visual effect in the gallery must be anticipated and mapped out to ensure the visitor's pleasure. The amount of works to be seen cannot be too much (and tire the visitor) or too little (and leave him unsatisfied).

The great restaurateur, Fernand Point (1897–1955) created a harmony of the senses, trying to delight our eyes and our ears, our nostrils, and our taste buds. The touch of fresh linen was as important as the bright sounds of a fine glass. The visual presentation of a dish was not a theatrical effect but his calculated effect to make you enjoy the food before you tasted it.

English Panelled Room
Benjamin West (1738-1820), *King Priam*, 1808
Tea and Coffee Service with Tray, Grogan Company
Sheraton Inlaid Swell Front Sideboard, Massachusetts, c. 1820

FRENCH MARKET SOUP

12 servings

In this soup, as with many French dishes, the simplest of ingredients produce a wonderful dish.

1 (12-ounce) package mixed dried beans
1 large onion, chopped
2 cloves of garlic, chopped
3 tablespoons olive oil
3 cups chicken stock
3 cups beef stock
1 smoked ham hock
1 whole chicken breast
1 (16-ounce) can chopped tomatoes
1/2 medium head cabbage, sliced diagonally
1/4 cup chopped parsley
Tabasco sauce to taste

Rinse and sort the beans. Soak in water to cover for 8 to 10 hours; drain. Set aside.

Sauté the onion and garlic in the oil in a large heavy stockpot until tender. Stir into the soaked beans with the stocks, ham hock, chicken, un-drained tomatoes and cabbage.

Cook, covered, on low for 6 hours.

Remove the ham hock and chicken. Cut the meat into bite-size pieces, discarding the bones. Add the meat to the soup with the parsley.

Reheat the soup. Add Tabasco sauce to taste. May sprinkle with your favorite grated cheese before serving.

Serve with a salad and fresh French or Italian bread. —*Sheila Quinn Smith*

Photograph on overleaf, English Panelled Room:

Sheraton Inlaid Swell Front Sideboard, Massachusetts, c. 1820; Rosewood and Satinwood; Length 70½ inches, depth 25½ inches, height 41 inches; Gift of Elizabeth Braun Ernst Estate by exchange.

Tea and Coffee Service with Tray, Grogan Company, Sterling Silver; Length of tray 29¾ inches; Gift of Mr. and Mrs. John Barclay.

Benjamin West (1738–1820), *King Priam*, 1808; Oil on canvas, 47x69¾ inches; Gift of William A. Coulter Fund.

CABBAGE SOUP

15 servings

1 ham bone
1/2 cup chopped ham
8 cups coarsely chopped
   cabbage
1 (16-ounce) can tomato
   purée
2 bay leaves
8 cups water
2 tablespoons sugar
1/4 teaspoon cracked
   pepper
Hot pepper sauce to taste

Combine the ham bone with ham, cabbage, purée, bay leaves, water, sugar, pepper and hot pepper sauce in a large stockpot.

Bring to a boil over high heat. Reduce heat to low. Simmer for 40 minutes or until the cabbage is tender, stirring frequently.

Discard the ham bone and bay leaves.
—*Tracy Morford*

LEEK AND POTATO SOUP

8 servings

Make this soup seem even richer by puréeing about half the cooked vegetables in a blender or food processor and then adding the milk. Be sure to stir frequently while heating to serving temperature.

6 leeks, white portions
   only, well washed
2 large onions, chopped
1/2 cup butter
3 cups cubed potatoes
6 cups chicken broth

2 cups milk
Salt and freshly ground
   pepper to taste
1 cup julienned ham
Finely chopped parsley
   to taste

Cut the leeks into slices. Sauté with the onions in butter in a stockpot until the onions are tender. Add the potatoes and broth.

Simmer, covered, for 30 minutes.

Stir in the milk. Cook just until heated through but not boiling. Season with salt and pepper.

Ladle into soup bowls. Sprinkle with the ham and parsley. —*Summer Friedlander*

EGGPLANT SALAD ROMANIAN-STYLE

6 servings

Beautiful and healthful! Serve on a white plate beside a small bed of leaf lettuce with rye bread and butter.

1 large firm eggplant
2 tablespoons olive oil
Coarse salt
Salt and pepper to taste
3 cloves of garlic
1/4 cup extra-virgin olive oil

1/2 tomato, chopped
1/2 cup chopped sweet onion
1/2 green bell pepper, chopped
1/2 red bell pepper, chopped
1/2 cup cucumber, seeded, peeled, chopped
2 tablespoons fresh lemon juice
1/2 teaspoon red wine vinegar or Balsamic vinegar

Preheat the oven to 350 degrees.

Coat the eggplant with 2 tablespoons olive oil. Pierce the eggplant 3 or 4 times with a sharp knife. Sprinkle with the coarse salt. Place in a shallow baking pan. Bake at 350 degrees for 1 to 1 1/4 hours or until tender.

Peel the eggplant and chop finely. Sprinkle with salt and pepper. Spoon the eggplant into a 1-quart jar with a tight-fitting lid.

Squeeze the garlic through a press into the olive oil. Pour over the chopped eggplant. Chill, tightly covered, overnight.

Combine the eggplant with the tomato, onion, bell peppers, cucumber, lemon juice and vinegar in a large bowl; toss well. —*Aaronel deRoy Gruber*

Place the unpeeled core of garlic in garlic press. Squeeze. Scrape garlic off press with the back of the knife. Remove the skin from the press. This will automatically clean your garlic press.

LEMON POTATO SALAD

10 servings

Serve this refreshing salad in a glass bowl with lemon twists and additional sprigs of mint for garnish.

6 red or white potatoes
  (about 3 pounds)
2 cups chopped celery
  with heart and inside
  leaves
2 cups broccoli florets
1 cup thinly sliced
  Vidalia onion
2 carrots, sliced
2 small tomatoes,
  seeded, chopped

2 cups mayonnaise
2/3 cup lemon juice
3 tablespoons (or more)
  chopped fresh mint
1 teaspoon salt
1 teaspoon pepper

Cook the unpeeled potatoes in water to cover in a saucepan until tender; drain and cool.

Peel the potatoes and cut into cubes. Combine with the celery, broccoli, onion, carrots and tomatoes in a bowl.

Combine the mayonnaise, lemon juice, mint, salt and pepper in a small bowl; mix well.

Add the dressing to the salad; toss gently to mix. Chill until serving time. —*Lee Wood*

SHERRIED POT ROAST

6 servings

The sauce makes the roast wonderful.

14x20-inch cooking bag
1/2 cup dry sherry
1/4 cup soy sauce
1/4 cup water
3 cloves of garlic, minced
1 teaspoon dry mustard
1 teaspoon thyme,
  crushed
1/4 teaspoon ground
  ginger
1/8 teaspoon freshly
  ground pepper
2 tablespoons flour
1 (2 1/2-pound) chuck
  roast

Preheat the oven to 325 degrees.

Combine the sherry, soy sauce, water, garlic, dry mustard, thyme, ginger and pepper in a bowl.

Place the flour in the cooking bag; shake well. Add the sherry mixture; shake well. Place the roast in the cooking bag; seal and slit the top for ventilation. Place the cooking bag in a shallow baking pan.

Bake at 325 degrees for 2 1/2 to 3 hours. Let stand for 15 minutes before slicing. May microwave on Medium for 1 hour. —*Becky Henry*

TOURNEDOS ROSSINI

6 servings

Rossini was a composer, but he immortalized French cuisine with his tournedos and foie gras. In Italy, truffles and truffle juice are used in the sauce.

6 (1-inch thick)
    center-cut filets
    mignons
Salt and freshly ground
    pepper to taste
1/4 cup unsalted butter
6 slices Italian bread,
    toasted
6 slices foie gras

2 tablespoons butter
1 cup thinly sliced
    mushrooms
1/2 cup port
1/2 cup beef broth
Greek seasoning to taste

Preheat the oven to 325 degrees.

Pound the filets with a wooden mallet to flatten slightly. Sprinkle with salt and pepper.

Heat 1/4 cup unsalted butter in a skillet. Cook the filets for 3 to 4 minutes, turning 1 time.

Arrange the toast on an ovenproof dish. Place a filet on each slice, reserving any remaining butter in the skillet. Top each filet with a slice of foie gras. Keep hot in oven while the sauce is prepared.

Add the remaining 2 tablespoons butter to the skillet. Sauté the mushrooms for 2 to 3 minutes. Stir in the port, broth, Greek seasoning, salt and pepper. Cook until heated through.

Spoon the mushroom sauce over the filets. Serve immediately.

May substitute burgundy for the port if preferred.
—*Isabel Haggerson*

BEEF BARLEY VEGETABLE STEW

6 servings

The stew improves in flavor if made a day in advance, cooled, chilled and reheated.

1 cup dried red kidney
    beans
4 cups chicken stock
4 cups beef stock
1 pound beef chuck, cut
    into 1 1/2-inch chunks
1/4 cup pearl barley
1 small onion, chopped
1 small potato, chopped
1 small carrot, chopped

Rinse and sort the beans. Combine with the stocks, beef, barley, onion, potato and carrot in a large saucepan.

Bring to a boil, skimming any foam as it rises. Reduce heat to low. Simmer for 4 hours. Add additional stock or water if needed to keep the vegetables covered.

A low-sodium broth may be used if a less salty taste is preferred. —*Nancy B. Jamison*

SUGAR HILL MEAT LOAF

6 servings

3 slices Italian bread
1/2 cup milk
2 tablespoons chopped
  onion
1 large clove of garlic,
  chopped
2 tablespoons butter
1½ pounds ground
  round, ground 2 times
1 teaspoon salt
1/8 teaspoon pepper
1/8 teaspoon Mrs. Dash
  spicy seasoning
Nutmeg to taste
1/4 cup chopped parsley
1/2 teaspoon
  Worcestershire sauce
2 eggs, lightly beaten
2 teaspoons virgin olive
  oil
1/4 cup granulated light
  brown sugar

Preheat the oven to 325 degrees.

Soak the bread in the milk in a bowl.

Sauté the onion and garlic in butter in a skillet until the onion is tender. Set aside.

Place the beef in a large bowl. Add the soaked bread, mixing well. Stir in the salt, pepper, spicy seasoning, nutmeg, parsley and Worcestershire sauce with a fork. Add the sautéed onion mixture, eggs and oil; mix well.

Shape into a loaf on a baking dish coated with nonstick cooking spray. Sprinkle with the brown sugar.

Bake at 325 degrees for 45 minutes.
—*Isabel Haggerson*

HAM LOAVES

10 to 12 servings

This is an old Thomas family recipe served on special occasions.

2 pounds ground pork
2 pounds ground ham
3 eggs
3/4 cup milk
1½ cups bread crumbs
2 cups packed brown
  sugar
1/2 cup water
1/4 cup vinegar
1 teaspoon prepared
  mustard

Preheat the oven to 375 degrees

Mix the ground pork and ham with the eggs, milk and bread crumbs in a large bowl. Shape into 2 loaves in baking dishes.

Combine the brown sugar with water, vinegar and mustard in a saucepan. Cook until heated through.

Bake the meat loaves, covered, at 375 degrees for 2 hours, basting every 15 minutes with the brown sugar sauce. —*Dee Thomas*

HERBED PORK TENDERLOINS

6 servings

Fresh herbs, if they are available, are even better for this simple but elegant dish. Substitute one tablespoon of the fresh herbs for one teaspoon of the dried.

1 teaspoon dried oregano
1 teaspoon dried basil
1 teaspoon dried
   rosemary
1 teaspoon dried thyme
1 teaspoon dried dill
1 teaspoon dried chives
1 teaspoon parsley flakes
1 clove of garlic, crushed
1/4 to 1/2 cup olive oil

2 (12-ounce) pork
   tenderloins
1/2 cup sherry

Combine the oregano, basil, rosemary, thyme, dill, chives, parsley and garlic in a blender container. Process until finely chopped. Add the olive oil gradually, processing constantly until smooth.

Place the pork in a shallow baking dish. Pour the herb mixture over the pork, turning to coat well. Marinate in the refrigerator for 8 hours or longer.

Preheat the oven to 325 degrees.

Pour the sherry over the pork in the baking dish. Roast the pork in the marinade for 30 to 35 minutes or until cooked through, basting frequently. —*Winnie Palmer*

VEAL SCALOPPINE WITH MARSALA

2 servings

Be sure to use the best veal it is possible to buy.

1/2 pound (1/4-inch thick)
   veal cutlet
2 tablespoons flour
Salt and freshly ground
   pepper to taste
2 tablespoons butter
2 tablespoons olive oil
1/4 cup marsala

Cut the veal into 3x3-inch pieces. Flatten with a wooden mallet between 2 sheets of waxed paper.

Blend the flour, salt and pepper together. Coat the veal lightly with the mixture.

Heat the butter and olive oil in a heavy skillet over high heat; do not let the butter brown. Cook the coated veal for 4 to 6 minutes or until golden brown on both sides. Keep warm on a serving plate.

Deglaze the skillet with the wine. Cook until reduced slightly. Pour over the cooked veal.
—*Isabel Haggerson*

CHICKEN ALMOND CASSEROLE

8 servings

The Brandied Peaches are an unusual and attractive complement.

4 large boneless chicken breasts, split
³/₄ cup flour
2 teaspoons (or less) salt
¹/₄ teaspoon pepper
1¹/₂ teaspoons paprika
¹/₂ cup butter

¹/₂ cup slivered almonds
1¹/₂ cups water
1 (10-ounce) can condensed beef consommé
2 tablespoons catsup
1 cup sour cream
1 cup grated Parmesan cheese

Preheat the oven to 350 degrees.

Rinse the chicken; pat dry. Coat the chicken with a mixture of flour, salt, pepper and paprika. Reserve any remaining flour mixture for the sauce.

Brown the chicken in the butter in a skillet. Place in a 3-quart casserole.

Brown the almonds lightly in the same skillet. Add the reserved flour. Stir in the water, consommé and catsup gradually.

Cook until the mixture thickens, stirring constantly. Remove from the heat. Stir in the sour cream. Pour over the browned chicken.

Bake at 350 degrees for 1 hour. Sprinkle with the Parmesan cheese. Bake for 10 minutes longer. Serve with Brandied Peaches (see below).

BRANDIED PEACHES

8 servings

2 (20-ounce) cans cling peach halves
³/₄ to 1 cup peach syrup
³/₄ to 1 cup brandy
¹/₂ cup cider vinegar
3 cinnamon sticks
1 tablespoon whole cloves

Drain the peaches, reserving the syrup. Place the peaches in a bowl.

Place ³/₄ to 1 cup of the reserved syrup in a saucepan. Add an equal or desired amount of brandy. Stir in vinegar, cinnamon and cloves.

Simmer for 5 minutes. Pour the mixture over the peaches. Let stand until cool. Chill for 24 hours or longer.

Drain the peaches before serving and stud each half with a clove. —*Susan Bowman*

CHICKEN CHILI

16 servings

This garnished, colorful chili may remind you of a Frederic Remington painting of the West—action-filled and vibrant.

6 tablespoons olive oil
1 large yellow onion, chopped
4 cloves of garlic, minced
2 red bell peppers, diced
2 jalapeños, seeded, minced
3 tablespoons chili powder
1½ teaspoons cumin seeds
1 teaspoon ground coriander
Cinnamon to taste

12 chicken breast fillets, cut into 1-inch cubes
2 (16-ounce) cans tomatoes in purée, chopped
1 (16-ounce) can black beans
1 (16-ounce) can chick-peas
1 cup beer

¼ cup grated unsweetened chocolate
Salt to taste

Sour cream
Sliced black olives and scallions
Avocado cubes
Grated Cheddar cheese

Heat 3 tablespoons of the olive oil in Dutch oven over medium heat. Add the onion and garlic. Cook for 2 minutes, stirring frequently.

Add the red peppers and jalapeños. Cook for 8 minutes, stirring frequently.

Stir in the chili powder, cumin seeds, coriander and cinnamon. Cook for 5 minutes. Remove from the heat.

Fry the chicken in batches in the remaining 3 tablespoons olive oil in a large saucepan.

Add the chicken, undrained tomatoes, black beans, chick-peas and beer to the Dutch oven; stir to mix well.

Cook over medium heat for 15 minutes. Stir in the chocolate; season with salt to taste.

Serve the chili with dollops of sour cream, sliced black olives and scallions, avocado cubes and grated Cheddar cheese. —*Melissa Rodgers*

Decorate your table or buffet with an array of the garnishes served in a combination of colorful and earthenware dishes for your guests to chose from.

CURRANT BREAST OF CHICKEN

6 servings

Such an easy way to get rave reviews. Serve this elegant company dish with wild rice

6 chicken breast halves
Salt and pepper to taste

1 (8-ounce) jar red
   currant jelly
1/2 cup water
1 tablespoon cornstarch
2 teaspoons allspice
1 tablespoon
   Worcestershire sauce
2 tablespoons lemon
   juice

Preheat the oven to 350 degrees.

Place the chicken in a greased baking pan. Sprinkle with salt and pepper.

Combine the jelly, water, cornstarch, allspice, Worcestershire sauce and lemon juice in a saucepan. Pour over the chicken.

Bake at 350 degrees for 1 hour, basting frequently.
—*Diana Jannetta*

CHICKEN MIRABELLE

8 servings

No one will recognize that the secret ingredient is prunes unless you tell.

8 chicken breast fillets
1/2 cup pitted prunes
4 cloves of garlic,
   crushed
1/4 cup dried oregano
1/4 cup red wine vinegar
1/4 cup olive oil
1/4 cup green olives
1/4 cup capers
3 bay leaves
1/2 cup packed brown
   sugar
1/2 cup white wine

Preheat the oven to 350 degrees.

Arrange the chicken in a shallow baking dish.

Process the prunes in the bowl of a food processor until puréed. Combine with the garlic, oregano, vinegar, olive oil, olives, capers, bay leaves, brown sugar and wine. Spoon over the chicken.

Bake, covered, at 350 degrees for 1 hour. Remove the bay leaves. Serve with a sprinkling of fresh parsley. —*Barbara L. Childs*

POLLO AL PARMIGIANA

4 servings

4 chicken breast fillets
1 cup grated Parmesan
  cheese
6 tablespoons butter
3 cloves of garlic, minced

2 tablespoons flour
1 cup chicken stock
½ cup white wine
1 cup medium
  mushrooms
Salt and pepper to taste

Preheat the oven to 350 degrees.

Rinse the chicken; pat dry. Coat the chicken with the Parmesan cheese.

Melt the butter in a skillet. Sauté the garlic and chicken for 10 minutes, turning the chicken 1 time. Place in a baking dish; keep warm.

Drain the butter from the skillet, reserving 2 to 3 tablespoons. Stir in the flour. Add the stock and wine, stirring constantly.

Add the mushrooms, salt and pepper. Cook over low heat for 10 to 12 minutes or until thickened, stirring frequently. Pour over the chicken.

Bake at 350 degrees for 30 minutes. Garnish with parsley. —*Michaelene McWhinney*

When cooking with wine, allow enough time for the alcohol to evaporate—about 2 minutes for white wine in a shallow skillet. Otherwise the dish will taste harsh. Reduce red wine by 50%—white wine a little more.

Rolled Chicken Fillets

6 servings

This unusual and adaptable recipe originated in Africa, where "ground nuts" are a common ingredient. Serve a side dish of rice or couscous and a salad with oil and vinegar dressing.

1/2 cup chopped candied
   ginger
1 cup white wine
6 boneless skinless
   chicken breast fillets
4 boneless skinless
   chicken thighs
2 tablespoons olive oil
Paprika to taste
Salt and pepper to taste
1 cup cold butter, cut
   into 1/2-inch pieces
1 pound dry-roasted
   skinless peanuts,
   ground

1 (10-ounce) can cream
   of chicken soup
1 cup chicken broth
1/2 cup chopped parsley

Preheat the oven to 350 degrees.

Combine the ginger and the wine in a small bowl. Set aside.

Rinse the chicken; pat dry. Flatten the chicken pieces with a wooden mallet. Rub the inside of the chicken pieces with olive oil. Sprinkle with paprika, salt and pepper. Top each with 1 piece of butter, 1 tablespoon of the ground peanuts and a small amount of the soaked ginger.

Roll up the chicken, tucking in the ends; secure with a wooden pick. Place in a greased 8x12-inch baking dish.

Sprinkle with paprika, salt and pepper. Top each with a piece of butter. Pour 1/2 cup of the wine over the top.

Bake at 350 degrees for 1 hour, basting every 20 minutes.

Combine the soup, broth and remaining 1/2 cup wine in a saucepan. Cook until heated through.

Stir in the remaining ground peanuts and 1/3 cup of the parsley. Pour the sauce over the hot chicken. Garnish with the remaining parsley.
—*Isabel Haggerson*

Chicken may be cut into smaller pieces, filled and rolled up similarly and served as an attractive hors d'oeuvre. Decrease the baking time appropriately.

CHICKEN SALTIMBOCCA

10 servings

10 boneless skinless
  chicken breast fillets
1/2 cup flour
1/2 cup butter
Salt and pepper to taste

2 tablespoons chopped
  shallot
2 cloves of garlic,
  chopped
1 cup mushrooms, sliced
1 unpeeled tomato,
  seeded, chopped
1 red bell pepper,
  chopped
1 cup veal or chicken
  stock
1/2 cup chardonnay
2 teaspoons fresh
  oregano
2 teaspoons fresh basil
2 teaspoons fresh thyme
3 tablespoons cornstarch
1/2 cup water
1/2 cup dry sherry
1/2 cup whipping cream

3 to 4 ounces Swiss
  cheese, thinly sliced
3 to 4 ounces prosciutto,
  thinly sliced

Preheat the oven to 350 degrees.

Rinse the chicken; pat dry. Coat the chicken with the flour.

Reserve 2 tablespoons of the butter for sautéing the vegetables. Melt the remaining butter in a skillet over medium heat.

Cook the chicken in the prepared skillet until browned. Place in a baking dish; sprinkle with salt and pepper.

Sauté the shallot and garlic in the reserved butter in a skillet. Add the mushrooms, tomato, bell pepper, stock, wine and herbs. Bring to a boil.

Dissolve the cornstarch in the water. Stir into the vegetable mixture. Cook until thickened, stirring constantly.

Stir in the sherry and whipping cream. Cook until heated through.

Layer 1 slice of the cheese and 1 slice of prosciutto over each chicken breast. Pour the sauce over the top.

Bake, covered, at 350 degrees for 30 minutes. Remove the cover. Bake for 10 minutes longer or until brown.

May substitute Gruyère or Emmentaler cheese for the Swiss cheese. —*Ernie Vallozzi*, **Vallozzi's**

ROAST LONG ISLAND DUCK

4 servings

1 (4- to 5-pound) duck
1 to 2 oranges, cut into
   quarters
1 medium onion, cut
   into quarters
1 carrot, cut into
   quarters
1 stalk celery, cut into
   halves
2 sprigs of parsley
Salt and freshly ground
   pepper to taste
Cherry Sauce (see below)

Rinse the duck inside and out; pat dry. Rub the duck inside and out with 1 orange quarter. Place in a baking pan. Place the remaining orange quarters, onion, carrot, celery, parsley and pepper in the duck cavity; truss. Sprinkle outside of the duck with salt and pepper.

Roast at 425 degrees for 45 to 60 minutes, turning frequently and discarding the pan drippings frequently. Reduce oven temperature to 400 degrees. Roast for 35 to 40 minutes longer or until golden brown and cooked through, discarding the pan drippings frequently.

Remove the duck to a platter; cut into quarters. Spoon a small amount of the Cherry Sauce onto 4 plates; top with the duck. Garnish the duck with additional parsley sprigs, a twisted thin slice of orange and cherries. Pass the remaining Cherry Sauce with the duck. Serve with wild rice and a green vegetable.

CHERRY SAUCE

1/2 cup sugar
1 1/2 tablespoons
   cornstarch
1/4 teaspoon salt
2 tablespoons wine
   vinegar
2/3 cup cherry juice
2 tablespoons lemon
   juice
1 1/2 cups pitted bing
   cherries

Combine the sugar, cornstarch and salt in a saucepan; mix well. Stir in the wine vinegar and cherry juice. Cook over low heat until thickened, stirring constantly. Stir in the cherries and lemon juice. Cook just until heated through, stirring occasionally.

May substitute raspberries for the cherries and orange juice for the cherry juice. Drizzle leftover sauce over ice cream or yogurt. May freeze for future use. —*Audrey Stern*

CHICKEN WITH CHARRED HOT PEPPERS

5 servings

Keep in mind that the volatile oil of the peppers is released in the air while the peppers are cooking and you will need good ventilation. A salad of mandarin oranges, bananas and strawberries on lettuce complements this nicely.

3/4 pound boneless
  skinless chicken
  breasts

1 tablespoon soy sauce
1 tablespoon cornstarch
1 1/2 tablespoons rice
  wine or dry sherry
1 egg white
3/4 teaspoon salt

1 tablespoon cornstarch
1 tablespoon rice wine
  or dry sherry
3 tablespoons soy sauce
1 1/2 teaspoons vinegar
2 teaspoons sugar

5 to 7 dried red hot
  peppers
5 tablespoons peanut oil
1 large red bell pepper,
  cut into 1-inch pieces
1 tablespoon finely
  chopped gingerroot
3/4 pound broccoli,
  broken into small
  florets
1/3 cup cashews, lightly
  toasted

Rinse the chicken; pat dry. Cut the chicken into 1-inch pieces.

Mix the 1 tablespoon soy sauce, 1 tablespoon cornstarch, 1 1/2 tablespoons rice wine, egg white and salt in a medium bowl.

Marinate the chicken in the soy sauce mixture for 15 minutes or longer.

Mix 1 tablespoon cornstarch, 1 tablespoon rice wine, 3 tablespoons soy sauce, vinegar and sugar in a small bowl. Set aside.

Remove the ends from the dried peppers and discard the seeds. Cut the peppers into 1-inch pieces.

Heat the peanut oil in a wok over medium heat. Cook the dried peppers just until lightly charred. Increase heat to high. Cook until the peppers are blackened.

Stir 1 tablespoon of the hot oil into the chicken pieces. Add the chicken pieces to the wok. Reduce the heat to medium. Stir-fry until the chicken begins to turn white. Add the bell pepper, gingerroot and broccoli. Stir-fry for a few seconds longer.

Add the cashews and seasoning mixture. Stir-fry for 15 seconds.

Serve immediately over hot rice. —*Linda Austin*

CHICKEN CURRY

10 servings

For a lovely fall dish, serve the condiments in pumpkin bowls (which need to be prepared in advance).

3/4 cup unsalted butter
2 large onions, chopped
3 stalks celery, chopped
3 large cloves of garlic, minced
1/4 cup chopped fresh parsley
2 bay leaves
1 (1-inch) piece gingerroot, peeled, minced
3 tart apples, peeled, diced
2 pears, peeled, diced
1 teaspoon dry mustard
1/2 teaspoon crushed red pepper flakes

3/4 pound ham, diced
5 tablespoons flour
2 teaspoons mace
1/4 cup (about) curry powder
1 teaspoon salt
5 cups chicken stock

3 large boneless skinless chicken breasts, cut into 1-inch cubes
6 tablespoons cream of coconut
3/4 cup golden raisins

Pumpkin Bowls (page 115)
Curry Condiments (page 115)

Melt the butter in a large stockpot. Add the onions, celery, garlic, parsley, bay leaves, gingerroot, apples, pears, dry mustard and crushed pepper flakes.

Cook over medium heat for 10 minutes or until the vegetables are very soft.

Add the ham, stirring until coated with butter. Stir in the flour, mace, curry powder and salt. Cook over medium-low heat for 5 minutes, stirring frequently.

Stir in the stock. Bring just to a boil over medium-high heat. Reduce heat to low. Simmer for 1 hour.

Remove the bay leaves. Spoon half the solids into a food processor container, using a slotted spoon. Process until smooth. Return to the stockpot; stir.

Add the cubed chicken. Simmer for 8 to 10 minutes or until the chicken is cooked through.

Stir in the coconut cream and raisins. Serve over hot cooked white rice and with the Curry Condiments.

Granny Smith apples are a good choice for use in this recipe. Be sure the pears are well ripened, but not soft.

Curry Condiments in Pumpkin Bowls

The vegetables may be prepared ahead, placed in bags and chilled in the refrigerator. Fill the pumpkin bowls just before serving.

8 to 12 small pumpkins
  (6 to 8 inches in
  diameter)

2 or 3 red bell peppers
2 or 3 green bell peppers
2 or 3 bunches scallions
  with green tops
1 or 2 large red onions
2 or 3 firm ripe tomatoes
1/2 to 3/4 pounds peanuts
1/2 to 3/4 pounds cashews
2 cups golden raisins
1 (8 1/2-ounce) jar Major
  Grey's chutney
1 cup apple chutney
1 cup peach chutney

Cut the tops off the pumpkins in order to form bowls; discard the tops. Remove and discard the seeds or reserve to toast and serve as an additional condiment. Drain the pumpkin bowls upside down for 2 days.

Dry the inside of the pumpkins with paper towels. Line the pumpkins with foil or plastic wrap.

Dice the red and green peppers into a uniform size. Place the red peppers in one of the pumpkins and the green peppers in another.

Slice the scallions and arrange in another of the pumpkins.

Chop the red onions and place in one of the pumpkins.

Peel and seed the tomatoes and cut into small uniform pieces. Place in one of the pumpkins.

Fill the remaining pumpkins with the peanuts, cashews, raisins, Major Grey's chutney, apple chutney and peach chutney.

Arrange the filled pumpkins so that the condiments are available, allowing the diners to add condiments to the curry servings to suit individual tastes. —*Vicki Booher*, **Mountain View Inn**

CAJUN CRAB CAKES

8 servings

The consistency of these crab cakes is meant to be somewhat loose. They may be a bit challenging to work with, but they are well worth the effort.

2 pounds lump crab meat
1 cup soft bread crumbs
1 cup mixed red, green
   and yellow bell
   peppers, finely
   chopped
1 teaspoon Dijon
   mustard
2 drops of Tabasco sauce
1 dash of
   Worcestershire sauce
4 eggs
Salt to taste
Freshly ground pepper
   to taste
Clarified butter or
   vegetable oil for frying
Piquant Sauce
   (see below)

Mix the crab meat and bread crumbs in a bowl. Add the bell peppers, mustard, Tabasco sauce, Worcestershire sauce, eggs, salt and pepper, stirring with a fork.

Pat the mixture into 4-inch cakes.

Fry the crab cakes in the clarified butter in a skillet until light golden brown on both sides.

Serve with the Piquant Sauce.

PIQUANT SAUCE

2 large shallots, minced
Several white
   peppercorns, crushed
1 bay leaf
1 cup white wine
1/4 cup whipping cream
1/2 cup cold butter, cut
   into slices

1 tomato, peeled,
   seeded, finely chopped
1 tablespoon minced
   fresh cilantro
Minced jalapeños to taste

Combine half the minced shallots with the peppercorns, bay leaf and wine in a small saucepan. Cook over medium heat until most of the liquid has evaporated. Discard the bay leaf.

Stir in the whipping cream. Cook until reduced by half.

Add the butter 2 or 3 slices at a time, whisking constantly until melted. Strain the mixture. Keep warm over low heat.

Combine the tomato with the cilantro, the remaining shallot and jalapeños in a bowl. Stir into the warm butter sauce.

—*Jo Ann Lightcap,* **The Kitchen Shelf**

BAKED LOBSTER TAILS

4 servings

An elegant way to serve and eat lobster. The herbed butter is baked with the lobster.

4 (8-ounce) frozen
   lobster tails, thawed

¼ cup dry white wine
¼ teaspoon paprika
Cayenne to taste
4 sprigs of parsley
1 very thin slice of a
   small onion
1 sliver of garlic
¼ teaspoon salt
¼ cup butter, softened
1 slice light toast,
   broken into pieces

Preheat the oven to 350 degrees.

Cut through underside of the tails on both sides with kitchen shears. Remove the lobster meat from the tails; cut the meat into bite-size pieces, reserving the lobster tails. Refill the lobster tails with the chopped meat. Place in a baking pan.

Combine the wine, paprika, cayenne, parsley, onion, garlic, salt and butter in a food processor container. Process until smooth. Add the toast pieces, mixing to the consistency of whipped butter. Spread 1 to 2 tablespoons of the mixture over the meat.

Bake at 350 degrees for 20 minutes.
—*Sandra L. Cole*

TARRAGON ORANGE ROUGHY

4 servings

¼ cup orange juice
4 orange roughy fillets
2 tablespoons olive oil
   or safflower oil
1 tablespoon tarragon
1 tablespoon coarsely
   ground pepper
Grated rind of 2 oranges

Preheat the oven to 325 degrees.

Pour the orange juice into a shallow baking dish.

Brush the fish with the olive oil. Place in the baking dish.

Mix the tarragon, pepper and grated orange rind in a bowl. Sprinkle over the fish, patting lightly to form a crust.

Bake at 325 degrees for 20 to 25 minutes or until the fish feels slightly springy and looks opaque. Serve immediately. —*Summer Friedlander*

SALMON TANGO

3 servings

1/4 cup melted margarine
1/4 cup packed light
  brown sugar
1 tablespoon soy sauce
2 tablespoons lemon
  juice
2 tablespoons white wine

1 (1-pound) salmon fillet

Combine the margarine, brown sugar, soy sauce, lemon juice and wine in a bowl; mix well.

Place the salmon fillet on a piece of heavy-duty foil. Pour margarine mixture over the salmon. Fold the foil to enclose the salmon, sealing tightly. Place in a baking dish.

Marinate in the refrigerator for 30 minutes. Open the foil.

Preheat the oven to 400 degrees.

Bake the salmon for 30 minutes, basting occasionally. —*Berenice Pittler*

LA COSTA SALMON

4 servings

Salmon prepared in this manner is delicately flavored and low in fat.

Olive oil for coating
4 scallions, thinly sliced
1 (16-ounce) salmon
  fillet
5 tablespoons fresh
  lemon juice
6 mushrooms, thinly
  sliced
1 medium tomato,
  seeded, diced
2 tablespoons fresh dill
  or parsley

Preheat the oven to 400 degrees.

Cut a piece of foil 30 inches long; lay shiny side down. Spread the center area of the foil with olive oil. Sprinkle the oiled area with the scallion slices. Place the salmon on the scallions; sprinkle with the lemon juice.

Layer the mushrooms, tomato and dill over the top. Fold the remaining half of the foil over the salmon, pressing to seal the edges. Place the foil packet on a baking sheet.

Bake at 400 degrees for 20 minutes.

May prepare this recipe in advance and chill in the refrigerator until time to bake. Increase the baking time by 2 to 3 minutes. —*Sue Jamison*

GRILLED SHRIMP WITH PROSCIUTTO

6 servings

Basil and prosciutto, paired with shrimp, evoke delicious Mediterrean memories.

¾ cup dry white wine
¾ cup olive oil
¼ cup fresh lemon juice
2 tablespoons Dijon mustard
½ cup chopped fresh basil
Freshly cracked black peppercorns

24 jumbo shrimp with tails intact, peeled, deveined
24 large basil leaves
24 thin slices prosciutto

Combine the wine, olive oil, lemon juice, mustard, chopped basil and peppercorns in a bowl.

Place the shrimp in a shallow bowl. Pour the marinade over the top. Chill for 3 hours, turning occasionally.

Prepare the hot coals, using a generous amount of mesquite.

Remove the shrimp from the marinade, using a slotted spoon; reserve the marinade. Wrap the center of each shrimp with a basil leaf and a slice of prosciutto. Thread 4 shrimp lengthwise onto each of 6 metal skewers. Place the skewered shrimp over the hot coals.

Grill for several minutes on each side, basting frequently with the reserved marinade. Serve immediately. —*The Honorable Charles H. Loughran*

MEDITERRANEAN SHRIMP

4 servings

2 cloves of garlic, crushed
2 tablespoons olive oil
1 pound deveined shrimp
1 cup white wine
1 (16-ounce) can tomatoes, drained
¼ cup oil-cured black olives
¼ cup parsley
¼ teaspoon salt
Tabasco sauce to taste

Sauté the garlic in the olive oil in a skillet just until golden brown. Remove the garlic, using a slotted spoon; discard.

Sauté the shrimp in the same olive oil in the skillet just until the shrimp begin to turn pink. Remove the shrimp to a warm plate.

Add the wine. Bring to a boil over high heat. Boil for 5 minutes or until the liquid is reduced by ½.

Stir in the tomatoes, olives, parsley and salt. Cook for 5 minutes longer.

Add the cooked shrimp to the sauce. Cook until heated through. Stir in the Tabasco sauce.
—*Summer Friedlander*

Super Seafood Casserole

10 servings

This lovely casserole can be easily done ahead for a party and can also be prepared in individual ramekins or shells.

8 ounces fresh mushrooms, sliced
2 scallions, sliced
3 tablespoons butter
16 ounces shrimp, cut into bite-size pieces
8 ounces lump crab meat
8 ounces bay scallops or sea scallops, cut into halves
2 tablespoons lemon juice
3 tablespoons butter
3 tablespoons flour
2 tablespoons lemon juice

1/2 cup dry white wine
2 cups half-and-half
1 egg yolk, beaten
Salt and pepper to taste
1/2 cup chopped parsley

1/4 cup grated Parmesan cheese
1/2 to 3/4 cup fresh bread crumbs

Preheat the oven to 350 degrees.

Sauté the mushrooms with the scallions in 1 tablespoon of the butter in a skillet. Set aside.

Melt 2 tablespoons butter in a heavy skillet over high heat. Add the shrimp, crab meat, scallops and 2 tablespoons lemon juice. Cook for 3 minutes, tossing constantly. Drain the seafood mixture, reserving the liquid.

Melt 3 tablespoons butter in a saucepan over low heat. Add the flour. Cook for 3 minutes, stirring constantly. Add the reserved seafood liquid, remaining 2 tablespoons lemon juice and the wine, whisking constantly. Add the half-and-half gradually, whisking constantly until the sauce is of the consistency of thick cream.

Stir a small amount of the warm mixture into the beaten egg yolk; add the egg yolk to the warm mixture, whisking constantly. Add the salt and pepper as desired.

Stir in the cooked seafood, mushrooms and parsley. Spoon into a baking dish or ramekins. Prepare ahead to this point and chill or freeze.

Top with a mixture of Parmesan cheese and bread crumbs.

Bake at 350 degrees for 30 minutes for casserole, 15 to 20 minutes for ramekins. Defrost before baking if frozen. —*Sue Jamison*

SPAGHETTI CARBONARA

8 servings

A much more elegant dish than the nickname "bacon and eggs" pasta implies. This version is lower in fat than most because it does not use cream.

10 ounces pancetta or rindless bacon, finely diced
1 hot chile pepper, finely chopped

20 ounces uncooked spaghetti
6 tablespoons grated pecorino or Romano cheese
6 egg yolks
Salt and freshly ground pepper to taste
3 tablespoons freshly grated Parmesan cheese

Combine the pancetta and the chile pepper in a skillet. Cook over low heat until some of the fat has melted. Increase the heat. Cook until browned.

Cook the spaghetti al dente using package directions. Drain, reserving ½ cup of the cooking liquid. Place the spaghetti in a large bowl.

Combine the reserved cooking water and pecorino cheese. Add the egg yolks, mixing with a fork. Add salt and a generous amount of pepper.

Pour the pancetta, pan drippings and the egg mixture over the spaghetti; toss well. Spoon onto a serving platter. Sprinkle with Parmesan cheese. Serve immediately. —*Ernie Vallozzi*, **Vallozzi's**

Theory and experience are as one in proving that the quality and quantity of food consumed wields a powerful influence over work, rest, sleep and dreams. —Fernand Point (1897–1955), Restaurateur

DR. CHEW'S PUTTANESCA SAUCE

4 servings

If good flavorful fresh tomatoes are not available, use canned tomatoes. Three cans of whole tomatoes can be drained and squeezed and the juice reserved to adjust the thickness of the sauce. Do the vegetable preparations in advance if you wish, but do not cook the pasta or the sauce until just before serving time.

2 pounds fresh tomatoes

6 cloves of garlic, finely chopped
1 medium onion, chopped
1/4 cup virgin olive oil
1/2 small jalapeño, chopped
1 medium green bell pepper, chopped
1 medium red bell pepper, chopped

2/3 cup chopped black olives
1 (2-ounce) can anchovies, chopped
1/4 cup drained capers
2 teaspoons chopped fresh oregano
2 tablespoons chopped fresh basil
1/2 teaspoon pepper

20 ounces uncooked angel hair pasta
1 tablespoon virgin olive oil

Peel and chop the tomatoes, reserving the liquid to thin the sauce if needed.

Cook the garlic and onion in 1/4 cup olive oil in a large heavy skillet over medium heat for 10 minutes. Add the jalapeño and the bell peppers. Cook for 5 minutes longer.

Stir in the black olives, anchovies, capers, oregano, basil and pepper. Add the tomatoes. Simmer over low heat for 15 minutes.

Add reserved tomato liquid if needed for the desired consistency.

Cook the pasta al dente using the package directions. Toss the cooked pasta with 1 tablespoon olive oil. Place on serving plates; top with the sauce.

May substitute 1 teaspoon dried oregano and 1 teaspoon dried basil for the fresh oregano and basil. Use vermicelli instead of the angel hair pasta if desired. —*Dr. Paul A. Chew*

LINGUINI MARINARA

8 servings

Simply special, easy, light and healthful.

3 to 4 tablespoons olive
  oil
2 or 3 cloves of garlic,
  crushed
1 (28-ounce) can stewed
  tomatoes
1 (6-ounce) can tomato
  paste
1 tablespoon sugar
Salt and pepper to taste

1 (16-ounce) package
  linguini

Heat the olive oil in a saucepan. Sauté the garlic in the olive oil over medium heat until golden brown.

Add undrained tomatoes. Crush the tomatoes with a potato masher. Stir in the tomato paste, sugar, salt and pepper.

Simmer for 5 to 7 minutes or until the sauce is of the desired consistency.

Cook the linguini al dente using package directions. Spoon onto serving plates; top with hot tomato sauce. —*Wendy Morford*

TOMATO–TOMATO SAUCE

6 servings

Serve this capered tomato double-dose over fish or chicken as well as pasta.

1/4 cup sun-dried
  tomatoes
4 medium tomatoes,
  diced
1/4 cup diced red onion
1/4 cup chopped basil
1/4 cup drained capers
1 tablespoon minced
  garlic
1/2 cup olive oil
Pepper to taste

Reconstitute the sun-dried tomatoes in hot water; drain.

Combine the reconstituted tomatoes with the diced fresh tomatoes, onion, basil, capers, garlic, olive oil and pepper in a saucepan; mix well. Let stand for 20 minutes.

Cook the tomato mixture over low heat for 10 to 15 minutes or until of the desired consistency. Spoon into a sauceboat. —*Audrey Stern*

ASPARAGUS À LA ORANGE

6 servings

Serve this unusual recipe as a first course or side dish. If fresh tarragon is not available, use fresh basil.

1½ pounds asparagus
Salt

Grated peel of 1 orange
Juice of 1 orange
1 (1-inch) piece fresh
 gingerroot, peeled,
 minced
1 tablespoon fresh
 tarragon, chopped
Salt and pepper to taste

Trim the tough ends off the asparagus and pare lightly using a vegetable peeler.

Bring ½ inch lightly salted water to a boil in a large skillet. Add the asparagus. Cook for 3 to 5 minutes or until tender-crisp; drain. Refresh under cold water; drain.

Combine the grated orange peel, orange juice, gingerroot and tarragon; mix well. Pour over the asparagus. Season with salt and pepper.
—*Summer Friedlander*

CREAMED ASPARAGUS IN PASTRY SHELLS

6 servings

Rich enough to serve as a luncheon entrée, this puff pastry presentation also makes it ideal for buffets.

1 pound asparagus
Salt to taste

3 tablespoons butter or
 margarine
1 cup sliced mushrooms
2 tablespoons finely
 chopped onion
3 tablespoons flour
¼ teaspoon dry mustard
1 (10-ounce) can
 condensed chicken
 broth
½ cup sour cream
6 baked puff pastry
 shells

Cook the asparagus in ½ inch boiling salted water in a saucepan for 10 minutes or until tender-crisp. Remove half the asparagus; cut into 1-inch pieces. Set aside. Cook the remaining asparagus for 5 minutes longer. Drain and keep warm.

Melt the butter in a skillet. Add the mushrooms and onion; sauté until tender. Stir in the flour and dry mustard. Cook for 1 minute. Stir in the broth gradually. Cook until thickened, stirring frequently.

Stir the cut asparagus and the sour cream into the sauce. Cook until heated through. Spoon into baked puff pastry shells on serving plates. Serve with the asparagus spears. —*Lisa R. Moeller*

BEST–EVER BEETS

4 servings

For a holiday presentation, prepare the beets in a white porcelain quiche pan or baking dish. Do not try this recipe with pickled beets.

1 large onion, chopped
2 tablespoons butter
1 (14-ounce) can beets
2 tablespoons butter
1 cup dry bread crumbs
1 cup sour cream

Preheat the oven to 350 degrees.

Sauté the onion in 2 tablespoons butter in a skillet until tender.

Drain the beets, reserving 1 cup of the liquid. Chop the beets. Add the reserved liquid and the chopped beets to the onion in the skillet.

Melt the remaining 2 tablespoons butter in a small skillet. Sauté the bread crumbs in the butter until lightly browned, tossing frequently.

Add ⅔ of the browned bread crumbs to the onion and beet mixture, reserving the remainder for the topping.

Stir the sour cream into the beets. Spoon the mixture into a 9-inch quiche dish. Sprinkle with the reserved browned bread crumbs.

Bake at 350 degrees for 25 minutes.
—*Virginia Grosscup*

Garnish a salad with beet chips. Fresh beets may be peeled and frozen, then sliced (while frozen) paper thin. Blot dry and deep-fry in 350 degree oil until crisp, but not browned. Remove, drain and sprinkle lightly with salt.

NUTTED BROCCOLI WITH POPPY SEEDS

6 servings

A new sauce for a favorite vegetable.

Florets of 1 large bunch
   broccoli
2 tablespoons minced
   onion
2 tablespoons butter
1½ cups sour cream
1 teaspoon cider vinegar
2 teaspoons sugar
½ teaspoon paprika
½ teaspoon poppy seeds
¼ teaspoon salt
Cayenne to taste
⅓ cup chopped cashews

Steam the broccoli until of the desired degree of doneness. Keep warm on a heated platter.

Sauté the onion in the butter in a saucepan until tender. Remove from heat. Stir in the sour cream, vinegar, sugar, paprika, poppy seeds, salt and cayenne.

Cook until heated through but not boiling, stirring frequently. Spoon over the warm broccoli. Top with the cashews. —*Eve Novak*

MARINATED BROCCOLI

20 appetizer servings or
8 salad servings

The marinade for this dish works well with other vegetables.

3 bunches broccoli
1 cup cider vinegar
1 tablespoon sugar
1 tablespoon dillweed
1 tablespoon MSG
1 teaspoon salt
1 teaspoon coarsely
   ground pepper
1 teaspoon garlic salt
1½ cups vegetable oil

Cut the broccoli into small florets. Place in a large bowl.

Mix the vinegar with the sugar, dillweed, MSG, salt, pepper, garlic salt and oil in a bowl. Pour over the broccoli.

Chill, covered, for 24 hours. Toss lightly several times during the marinating process.

Drain before serving. —*Ann MacDonald*

EGGPLANT TIAN

6 servings

This eggplant recipe is served at the Cranberry Moose Restaurant in Yarmouth Port, Massachusetts. Adjust this low-calorie version by sautéing the eggplant in olive oil and by drizzling olive oil over the top before baking.

2 medium eggplant
Salt
2 medium onions
1 tablespoon olive oil
1 (14-ounce) can chunky
    tomatoes
Pepper to taste
1/2 cup grated Parmesan
    cheese

Cut the unpeeled eggplant into 1/2-inch rounds. Sprinkle both sides with salt. Drain on paper towels for 30 minutes.

Cut the onions into halves vertically. Cut the halves into thick slices. Sauté the sliced onions in olive oil in a skillet until lightly browned. Remove to a warm plate.

Preheat the oven to 400 degrees.

Rinse the eggplant rounds and dry with paper towels. Fry the eggplant in a skillet coated with nonstick cooking spray over medium heat until golden brown on both sides.

Grease a large baking dish with olive oil. Cook the tomatoes in a saucepan just until heated through.

Arrange half the eggplant in the prepared baking dish. Top with the sautéed onions. Season with salt and pepper. Sprinkle with half the Parmesan cheese. Layer the remaining eggplant, warmed tomatoes and remaining Parmesan cheese over the top. Spray the top with nonstick cooking spray.

Bake at 400 degrees for 30 to 40 minutes or until bubbly in the center. Let stand for several minutes before serving. —*Jerry L. Finegold*

If you like very spicy food, use the crushed red pepper-flavored variety of chunky tomatoes.

PEAS WITH CUCUMBER

5 servings

1 (10-ounce) package
    frozen peas
1 large peeled cucumber,
    seeded, chopped
1 chicken bouillon cube,
    crushed

Combine the frozen peas, cucumber and bouillon powder in a heavy saucepan. Let stand until the peas thaw.

Cook over high heat just until heated through, tossing constantly. Serve immediately.
—*Eve Novak*

NEW POTATOES A LA SMITONE

6 servings

Rich and delicious, these potatoes require about half the time to cook as a casserole.

1 pound small new red
    potatoes, cut into
    eighths
1 chicken bouillon cube

5 scallions, thinly sliced
1 cup sour cream
1/2 teaspoon garlic
    powder
1 1/2 tablespoons
    seasoned salt
2 tablespoons (or less)
    freshly ground pepper
1/3 cup freshly grated
    Parmesan cheese

Place the potatoes and bouillon cube in a saucepan. Add enough water to cover the potatoes by 1 inch. Boil for 7 to 10 minutes or until the potatoes are done to taste; drain.

Add the scallions, sour cream, garlic powder, seasoned salt and pepper; mix well. Add the Parmesan cheese; toss until covered. Serve immediately. —*Marquis M. Smith III*

STEAMED NEW POTATOES WITH GARLIC

4 servings

Simple, elegant and a perfect complement for beef or lamb.

12 to 16 small new
  potatoes
1 clove of garlic, sliced
  lengthwise
1 tablespoon chopped
  fresh parsley

Cut a small strip of the peel from around the center of each potato. Place the potatoes interspaced with garlic in a steamer basket over simmering water in a saucepan. Steam, covered, for 20 minutes or until the potatoes test done.

Remove the garlic. Spoon into a serving dish; sprinkle with the parsley. —*Linda Austin*

SPAGHETTI SQUASH PARMESAN

8 servings

This subtle, delicious side dish goes well with any entrée that is not strongly seasoned.

1 (1½-pound) spaghetti
  squash

½ cup butter
6 tablespoons flour
2 chicken bouillon cubes
½ cup hot water
2 cups milk
½ cup grated Parmesan
  cheese
Salt and pepper to taste

2 tablespoons grated
  Parmesan cheese

Preheat the oven to 350 degrees.

Place the squash on a baking sheet. Bake at 350 degrees for 1 hour or until tender. Cut the squash into halves, discarding the seeds. Separate the strands with a fork and set aside, discarding the squash shells.

Melt the butter in a heavy saucepan. Whisk in the flour. Cook over low heat for 5 minutes, whisking constantly. Dissolve the bouillon cubes in the hot water. Add to the saucepan. Whisk in the milk gradually. Cook for 10 minutes or until thickened, whisking constantly.

Whisk in ½ cup cheese, salt and pepper. Add the desired amount of squash strands; mixture should be somewhat creamy. Spoon into a buttered 10x12-inch baking dish. Top with the remaining 2 tablespoons cheese.

Bake at 350 degrees for 30 minutes or until bubbly and golden brown. —*Sue Jamison*

CANDIED SWEET POTATOES

6 servings

If you love sweet potatoes, you'll savor this version with spices and vanilla.

2 tablespoons butter or margarine
1/2 cup sugar
2 tablespoons (or more) water
1/2 teaspoon cinnamon
1/4 teaspoon nutmeg
1/2 to 3/4 teaspoon vanilla extract

4 large sweet potatoes, boiled, peeled, cut into halves
1 1/2 cups miniature marshmallows

Preheat the oven to 350 degrees.

Combine the butter, sugar, water, cinnamon, nutmeg and vanilla in a saucepan. Cook over low heat until the butter melts and the sugar dissolves, stirring constantly.

Add the sweet potatoes, turning to coat well. Cook until the sweet potatoes are glazed, adding additional water if necessary. Spoon into a large baking dish; pour any remaining glaze over the top.

Bake, covered, at 350 degrees for 30 minutes. Uncover; top with the marshmallows. Bake just until the marshmallows are golden brown.
—*Audrey Stern*

TOMATO PUDDING

8 servings

2 cups bread cubes or croutons
1/2 cup melted margarine
1 (10-ounce) can tomato purée
1 cup packed light brown sugar
1/4 cup water
1/4 teaspoon salt

Preheat the oven to 325 degrees.

Toss the bread cubes with the melted margarine in a bowl. Spread in a baking dish.

Combine the tomato purée, brown sugar, water and salt in a saucepan. Simmer for 5 minutes. Pour over the bread cubes.

Bake, covered, at 325 degrees for 45 minutes.
—*Lila Swartz*

Stir–Fried Vegetables

6 servings

These beautiful and flavorful vegetables make a satisfying accompaniment to beef or chicken or may be featured as a vegetarian main dish.

2 tablespoons cornstarch
2 tablespoons water
1 tablespoon soy sauce
2 tablespoons toasted
  sesame seeds
4 green onions, sliced
1 cup (about) chicken
  stock

2 tablespoons (or more)
  vegetable oil
1 tablespoon minced
  garlic
3/4 cup sliced onion
2 tablespoons freshly
  grated ginger
3/4 cup half sliced carrots
1 1/2 cups fresh
  cauliflowerets
1 1/2 cups fresh broccoli
  florets
3/4 cup half slices
  zucchini
3/4 cup (1-inch) strips
  red and green bell
  peppers
1 1/2 cups fresh snow peas
3/4 cup sliced yellow
  squash

Dissolve the cornstarch in the water in a bowl. Add the soy sauce, sesame seeds, green onions and chicken stock; mix well.

Heat the oil in a wok or heavy skillet. Add the garlic, onion and ginger. Stir-fry for 30 seconds.

Add the carrots, cauliflower, broccoli, zucchini, bell peppers, peas and yellow squash in the order listed, stir-frying until tender-crisp.

Stir the cornstarch mixture and add to the wok. Cook until thickened, stirring constantly.

Serve over hot cooked brown rice.
—*Summer Friedlander*

CRANBERRY SALSA

6 cups

This dish is beautiful and delicious.

2 cups water
1/2 cup sugar
1 (12-ounce) package
   fresh cranberries

1 clove of garlic, minced
1 or 2 jalapeños, seeded,
   minced
1/3 cup chopped cilantro
3 scallions, minced
1/4 cup fresh lime juice
Tabasco sauce to taste
Salt and freshly ground
   pepper to taste
1/4 cup sugar

Combine water and 1/2 cup sugar in a saucepan. Bring to a boil. Reduce the heat. Add the cranberries. Simmer for 2 to 3 minutes or until tender but still firm. Rinse with cold water and drain.

Combine the cranberries with the garlic, jalapeños, cilantro, scallions, lime juice, Tabasco sauce, salt and pepper in a bowl; mix well with a wooden spoon. Stir in 1/4 cup sugar.

Store, covered, in the refrigerator. Serve at room temperature. —*Amy Stern*

PINEAPPLE SALSA

8 to 10 cups

To retain the texture and individual flavors, serve the salsa within one hour of preparation. Serve in the pineapple shell for a pretty presentation.

1 small pineapple
1 red bell pepper
1 yellow bell pepper
1 green bell pepper
1 poblano pepper or 2 to
   3 jalapeños, seeded,
   finely chopped
1 small red onion, finely
   chopped
1/2 cup chopped cilantro
   or fresh mint
Freshly ground pepper
   to taste
3 to 4 tablespoons lime
   juice

Cut the pineapple into halves, leaving the leaves intact. Remove the fruit with a grapefruit knife, leaving the shell halves intact. Reserve the shell. Cut the fruit into 1-inch pieces, discarding the core.

Cut the bell peppers into 1-inch pieces. Combine with the pineapple, chile pepper, onion, cilantro, pepper and lime juice in a bowl; mix gently.

Serve in the pineapple shells as a side dish with fish or chicken. You may add 1 tablespoon brown sugar if desired.
—*Amy Stern*

PINEAPPLE GRATIN

10 servings

A perfect companion with any ham dish.

2 tablespoons cornstarch
1/4 cup water
1 (20-ounce) can
    crushed pineapple
1/2 cup sugar
2 eggs, beaten
1 teaspoon vanilla extract
Cinnamon to taste
2 tablespoons (or less)
    butter

Preheat the oven to 350 degrees.

Dissolve the cornstarch in the water in a bowl. Add the undrained pineapple, sugar, eggs and vanilla; mix well.

Spoon into a buttered baking dish. Sprinkle with cinnamon; dot with butter.

Bake at 350 degrees for 55 to 60 minutes. Serve warm. —*Beth Searfoss*

MUSHROOMS FLORENTINE

6 servings

1 clove of garlic, chopped
4 tablespoons butter
1 pound mushrooms,
    sliced

3 (10-ounce) packages
    frozen chopped
    spinach, thawed,
    drained
1/4 cup chopped onion
4 tablespoons melted
    butter
1 teaspoon salt
Pepper to taste
1 cup shredded Cheddar
    cheese

Preheat the oven to 350 degrees.

Sauté the garlic in 4 tablespoons butter in a skillet. Remove and discard the garlic. Sauté the mushrooms in the same skillet.

Combine the spinach, onion, 4 tablespoons melted butter, salt and pepper in a bowl; mix well.

Spread the spinach mixture in a 10-inch shallow baking dish. Sprinkle with 1/2 of the cheese. Top with the mushroom mixture and the remaining cheese.

Bake at 350 degrees for 20 to 30 minutes or until heated through and the cheese is melted.
—*Nancy D. Clarke*

EASY MUSHROOM SAUCE

4 servings

Serve with steak, meat loaf or leg of lamb.

8 ounces fresh
  mushrooms, thinly
  sliced
1/4 cup butter
1 tablespoon Wondra
  flour
1/2 cup whipping cream
2 tablespoons sherry
1/4 teaspoon salt
1/8 teaspoon white pepper

Sauté the mushrooms in the butter in a medium nonstick skillet until light brown. Stir in the flour.

Add the cream gradually. Cook until thickened, stirring constantly.

Add the sherry, salt and pepper.
—*Isabel Haggerson*

MUSHROOM AND WILD RICE CASSEROLE

6 servings

1 cup uncooked wild
  and long grain rice
1/2 cup coarsely chopped
  onion
1/2 cup butter or
  margarine
1 pound fresh
  mushrooms, sliced
1 (10-ounce) can beef
  broth
Salt and pepper to taste

Preheat the oven to 350 degrees.

Sauté the rice and onion in the butter in a Dutch oven for 7 minutes or until golden brown. Add the mushrooms, beef broth, salt and pepper.

Bake, covered, at 350 degrees for 1 hour; stir after 45 minutes. —*Joan DeRose*

WILD RICE AND APRICOT STUFFING

6 servings

1/2 cup chopped dried
    apricots
5 cups chicken broth

3 tablespoons unsalted
    butter
2 medium onions, finely
    chopped
2 cups wild rice, rinsed,
    drained
1/2 cup slivered almonds,
    toasted
1/4 cup minced fresh
    parsley
1/2 to 1 teaspoon salt
1/4 teaspoon freshly
    ground pepper

Combine the apricots and enough chicken broth to cover in a bowl. Chill for 2½ hours.

Heat the butter in a saucepan until melted. Stir in the onions. Cook over medium to low heat for 10 minutes or until tender, stirring constantly; do not brown. Stir in the apricot mixture, remaining broth, wild rice, almonds and parsley. Bring to a boil; reduce heat.

Simmer, covered, for 45 minutes or until the rice is tender. Season with the salt and pepper. Spoon into a buttered baking dish. Bake, covered, at 325 degrees for 30 minutes. —*Eve Novak*

SAVORY HERBED RICE

10 servings

1/4 cup minced onion
1 clove of garlic, minced
5 tablespoons melted
    butter
2 cups uncooked rice
3 cups chicken broth
1 tablespoon minced
    parsley
1/2 teaspoon thyme
1 bay leaf
Cayenne to taste

Sauté the onion and garlic in the butter in a saucepan until tender but not brown. Stir in the rice. Add the broth, parsley, thyme, bay leaf and cayenne; mix well.

Simmer over low to medium heat for 17 minutes, stirring often. Discard the bay leaf before serving. —*Cynthia Busch*

ARNIE'S SPOON BREAD

8 servings

This tasty recipe—as much a side dish as a bread—comes from the home of Winnie and Arnold Palmer.

1 (16-ounce) can
  creamed corn
1 cup yellow cornmeal
3/4 cup milk
1/3 cup vegetable oil
3 eggs
1 teaspoon baking soda
1 (4-ounce) can chopped
  green chiles
1 cup grated Cheddar
  cheese
1/2 teaspoon salt

Preheat the oven to 375 degrees.

Combine the corn, cornmeal, milk, oil, eggs, baking soda, green chiles, cheese and salt in a bowl; mix well. Spoon into a greased 8x8-inch baking pan.

Bake at 375 degrees for 30 to 45 minutes or until set and golden brown.

Serve with turkey and ham. —*Winnie Palmer*

PARSNIP PURÉE

5 servings

6 to 7 parsnips,
  trimmed, cut into
  1-inch slices
Salt to taste
1/2 cup half-and-half
2 tablespoons butter
White pepper to taste

Combine the parsnips and salt with enough water to cover in a saucepan. Cook until tender; drain.

Process the parsnips in a food processor until puréed or put through a food mill.

Heat the half-and-half in a saucepan. Add the butter and puréed parsnips, beating until of the consistency of mashed potatoes.

Season with salt and white pepper.
—*Isabel Haggerson*

SWEET AND SPICY MUSTARD RING

24 servings

"Smashingly different" was the verdict at the first museum tasting. Serve it with ham, beef or smoked turkey.

2/3 cup sugar
2 tablespoons dry mustard
1/4 teaspoon salt
2/3 cup vinegar
1/3 cup water
4 eggs, beaten
1 envelope unflavored gelatin
1 tablespoon cold water
1 cup whipping cream, whipped

Mix the sugar, dry mustard and salt in a bowl. Add the vinegar, 1/3 cup water and eggs; mix well.

Soften the gelatin in 1 tablespoon cold water in a double boiler. Place over hot water and cook until gelatin dissolves. Stir in the egg mixture gradually. Cook until thickened and smooth, stirring constantly.

Chill until partially set. Fold in the whipped cream. Spoon into an 8-inch mold. Chill until set.

Unmold onto a serving plate. —*Ruth Cook*

CUCUMBER AND HONEY

4 servings

An unusual combination of textures and tastes, this goes well with grilled chicken.

1 large cucumber, thinly sliced
1 large onion, coarsely chopped
1/2 to 1 cup honey

Combine the cucumber and onion in a bowl; mix well. Pour the honey over the cucumber mixture, tossing to coat. Serve immediately for a crisp texture.

May store in the refrigerator for several weeks; vegetable texture will not be as crisp, but the flavor is still delicious. —*Charlotte B. Bailey*

FRESH BASIL PESTO

1½ to 2 cups

Serve as an accompainment to grilled chicken, drizzle over the top of a tomato sauce as an artistic garni, add to soups for additional flavor, serve as a dip with crusty French bread, or stuff into hollowed out cherry tomatoes.

2 cups lightly packed fresh basil leaves

2 cloves of garlic
2 tablespoons pine nuts
½ teaspoon salt
½ cup extra-virgin olive oil
½ cup freshly grated Parmesan cheese
2 tablespoons freshly grated Romano cheese
2 tablespoons (or less) unsalted butter

Stem large leaves and tear gently into smaller pieces to create a uniform size for measuring.

Combine the basil, garlic, pine nuts, salt and 2 tablespoons of the olive oil in a food processor container. Process until mixture is puréed and a lovely color of green. Add the remaining olive oil, Parmesan cheese, Romano cheese and butter. Process until blended. Serve at room temperature over hot cooked pasta or as a side dish.

Preserve summer by processing first 5 ingredients in a food processor. Ladle into jars and freeze. Thaw and add the cheeses, butter and 1 to 2 tablespoons hot water if needed for the desired consistency. —*George Austin*

The pleasures of the table are of all times and all ages of every country and of every day. They go hand in hand with all our other pleasures, outlast them and in the end console them for our loss.
—aphorism, Brillat Savarin (1755–1826)

PLAYTHINGS AND COOKIES

PLAYTHINGS AND COOKIES

A doll in a faded but elegant dress; a tiny teacup decorated with hand-painted flowers; a worn, but still study red fire truck; a teddy bear with one arm worn by years of holding; the aroma of spices or the flaky sweet crunch of a sugar cookie...memories evoked of those special times of childhood.

Each year, from November to January, antique toys and trains are displayed at the Museum. These playthings, from the 19th and 20th centuries, offer a delightful transport backward into childhood's yesteryears. They also form a light-hearted and insightful collection against which the art and culture of their period may be studied and understood.

The idea for the collection was sparked in 1958 with the discovery of a doll, dolls' clothing, children's books, and several sets of toy dishes among the effects of the estate of the Museum's founder, Mary Marchand Woods. In 1968, the first toy exhibition was held with about 100 objects. As Dr. Paul Chew directed the selection and acquisition of toys, the size and value of the collection has grown. It includes a wide variety of treasures from Cracker Jack prizes to Lionel trains and pedal cars, from bisque dolls to Barbies and lunch boxes. Each year when the Museum opens its "toy chest," the event is celebrated with the serving of punch and cookies to children of all ages.

Doll's Tea Party
Girl Doll, c. 1900
"Floradora" Girl Doll, c. 1901-1930
Girl Doll, c. 1913

ALMOND MACAROONS

75 macaroons

This is a famous Greensburg recipe that originated at Mitinger's Ice Cream Shop, which operated on Main Street from the 1870s to 1922. The cookies are best one to two days after baking—if they last that long!

5½ fluid ounces of egg
    whites
2 cups sugar
1 (1-pound) block
    almond paste

Preheat the oven to 365 to 370 degrees.

Beat the egg whites into the sugar in a large mixer bowl. Break the almond paste into small pieces and add to the egg mixture. Beat at medium speed, rotating often, for 5 minutes or until of a thick and creamy texture with no lumps.

Cut 2 sheets of heavy non-recycled brown paper the size of a baking sheet; layer both on a nonstick baking sheet. Drop the macaroon mixture by rounded 1½ teaspoonfuls 1 inch apart onto the paper-covered baking sheet.

Bake on the middle oven rack at 365 to 370 degrees for 15 minutes or until light golden brown.

Remove the top brown paper with the cookies to a wire rack and cool for 5 minutes. Invert the paper and dampen the underside with a wet sponge or cloth. Remove the cookies and place right side up on the wire rack to cool for 15 to 20 minutes longer. —*Joe Mitinger*

Left overleaf, *Doll's Tea Party*

(from left to right):

Girl Doll, c. 1900; Armand Marseille, Koppelsdorf, Thuringia, Germany; Height 22 inches; Gift of Mr. and Mrs. Ralph H. Demmler.

Floradora Girl Doll, c. 1901–1930; Height 20 inches; *Gift of* the Estate of Mary Ann Zimmerman.

Girl Doll, c. 1913; Height 19½ inches; Gift of Mr. and Mrs. Ralph Demmler.

BARBIE™-HAS-MY-HEART COOKIES

48 cookies

The **Art In The Kitchen** *Cookbook Committee created this dark chocolate cookie recipe especially for the Barbie's 35th Birthday Celebration at Westmoreland Museum in October of 1994. The recipe also would make a pretty valentine cookie.*

1 cup butter-flavor
   shortening
1½ cups sugar
2 eggs
4 (1-ounce) squares
   unsweetened baking
   chocolate, melted
½ teaspoon rum extract
3 cups cake flour
2½ teaspoons baking
   powder
½ teaspoon salt
2 tablespoons milk
1 cup finely ground
   toasted almonds

½ cup raspberry
   preserves
¼ cup sifted
   confectioners' sugar

Cream the shortening and sugar in a large mixer bowl until light and fluffy. Add the eggs 1 at a time, mixing well after each addition. Stir in the slightly cooled chocolate and rum extract. Combine the flour, baking powder and salt in a small bowl. Add to the chocolate mixture alternately with the milk, mixing well after each addition until a stiff dough forms. Mix in the almonds.

Chill, covered, for 1 hour.

Preheat the oven to 375 degrees.

Divide the dough into 6 portions. Roll 1 portion at a time ⅛ inch thick on a floured surface using a floured rolling pin. Cut with a 2- to 2½-inch heart-shaped cookie cutter. Place the hearts on ungreased nonstick baking sheets. Spread ½ teaspoon preserves in the center of each heart.

Cut additional 2- to 2½-inch hearts and cut out the center portions of these hearts with a ½- to 1-inch heart-shaped cookie cutter.

Place the large hearts over the preserves; press the 2 cookies' edges together gently. Repeat rolling, cutting and assembling with remaining cookie dough and preserves.

Bake at 375 degrees for 10 to 12 minutes. Let stand on the baking sheet for 1 minute before removing to wire racks to cool completely. Sprinkle the edges with confectioners' sugar.

May fill a decorator tube fitted with a writing tip with white icing and pipe a "B" on the preserves in the center of each cookie.
—*Art In The Kitchen Cookbook Committee*

BLACK WALNUT REFRIGERATOR COOKIES

48 cookies

An old Pennsylvania Dutch recipe. Many Pennsylvania farms had several black walnut trees. Today, these prized walnuts are available at specialty food stores and farm markets.

1 cup butter or
    margarine, softened
1 teaspoon vanilla extract
2 cups packed brown
    sugar
2 eggs, beaten
3/4 cup black walnuts,
    finely chopped

2 1/2 cups plus 1
    tablespoon flour
1 teaspoon baking soda
1 teaspoon salt

Cream the butter and vanilla in a large mixer bowl until well blended. Add the brown sugar 1/2 cup at a time, beating after each addition until light and fluffy. Add the eggs gradually, beating well after each addition. Stir in the walnuts by hand.

Combine the flour, baking soda and salt in a small bowl. Add to the walnut mixture 1/2 cup at a time, stirring by hand after each addition.

Shape the dough into 1 1/2x7-inch logs. Wrap each log in waxed paper and chill for 4 to 24 hours or until firm.

Preheat the oven to 350 degrees.

Remove 1 log at a time from the refrigerator and cut into thin slices. Place the slices 1/2 inch apart on a nonstick baking sheet.

Bake at 350 degrees for 8 minutes.

Repeat the process with each log.

May substitute finely chopped toasted English walnuts for the black walnuts. —*Win Beidler*

BLONDIES

30 squares

Serve these light-colored brownies on a dark serving plate for a striking contrast.

2 cups flour
1 teaspoons baking
   powder
1 teaspoon salt

1/2 cup butter, softened
1 cup packed light
   brown sugar
1 cup sugar
4 extra-large eggs

2 teaspoons vanilla
   extract
1/2 teaspoon nutmeg
1/2 teaspoon cinnamon

2 cups semisweet
   chocolate chips
1 cup chopped pecans

Preheat the oven to 350 degrees.

Combine the flour, baking powder and salt in a small bowl; set aside.

Beat the butter in a large mixer bowl until light and fluffy. Add the brown sugar and sugar 1/2 cup at a time, beating well after each addition.

Add the eggs 1 at a time, mixing well after each addition.

Combine the vanilla, nutmeg and cinnamon in a small bowl; blend into the sugar mixture.

Add the flour mixture 1/2 cup at a time, beating well after each addition. Stir in half the chocolate chips and half the pecans.

Spread the mixture in a greased and floured 9x13-inch glass baking dish. Sprinkle the remaining chocolate chips and pecans over the top.

Bake at 350 degrees for 25 to 35 minutes or until a wooden pick inserted in the center comes out clean; do not overbake.

Let stand until cool. Cut into squares. These are great with vanilla ice cream. —*Sande Hendricks*

The combination of vanilla extract, nutmeg and cinnamon in this recipe is known as "Mexican Vanilla", and is sold only in Mexico. Those are the secret ingredients that give this recipe its unique flavor.

DECADENT BROWN SUGAR SQUARES

12 squares

Indulge yourself in the rich, delicious taste and savory texture of this dessert. Great for a luncheon or tea.

1/2 cup butter, cut into pieces and softened
3/4 cup firmly packed dark brown sugar
1 cup sifted flour

3/4 cup firmly packed dark brown sugar
2 tablespoons flour
1/2 teaspoon baking powder
1/4 teaspoon salt
2 eggs
1 teaspoon vanilla extract
1 cup chopped pecans

Preheat the oven to 300 degrees.

Cream the butter and half the brown sugar in a food processor. Add the 1 cup sifted flour one-third at a time, processing after each addition. Spread the mixture evenly in an ungreased 8-inch square baking pan.

Bake at 300 degrees for 20 minutes.

Remove the pan from the oven; increase the oven temperature to 350 degrees.

Process the remaining brown sugar, 2 tablespoons flour, baking powder and salt in the food processor until well mixed. Add the eggs 1 at a time, processing after each addition. Stir in the vanilla and pecans. Spread the mixture over the baked layer.

Bake at 350 degrees for 25 minutes.

Remove to a wire rack to cool. Cut into squares.
—*Marilee Grosscup Matteson*

Tea parties are another novelty, and provide an unparalled form of conversation, on that, being offered to persons who have already dined well, it supposes neither appetite nor thirst and has no end but distraction, nor any basis but its pleasant taste. —Brillat Savarin (1755–1826)

CHOCOLATE NUT WAFERS

60 wafers

This dessert has a wonderful chocolate flavor that's not too sweet. If you prefer, try using pecans, cashews or macadamia nuts.

1/2 cup butter, softened
1 cup sugar
2 eggs, beaten
2 (1-ounce) squares
  unsweetened baking
  chocolate, melted
1/4 teaspoon salt
1/2 teaspoon vanilla
  extract
2/3 cup flour
1 cup chopped walnuts

Preheat the oven to 350 degrees.

Cream the butter in a large mixer bowl. Add the sugar gradually, mixing well after each addition. Add the eggs; mix well. Add the chocolate, salt, vanilla and flour; mix until well blended. Stir in the walnuts.

Drop by teaspoonfuls 1 inch apart onto a greased cookie sheet.

Bake at 350 degrees for 8 to 10 minutes. Let cool on the cookie sheet for 1 minute before removing to a wire rack to cool completely.
—*Isabel Haggerson*

CINNAMON SQUARES

48 squares

Great served with hot chocolate on a cold day.

1 cup margarine,
  softened
1/4 cup packed brown
  sugar
3/4 cup sugar
4 teaspoons cinnamon
1 egg yolk
1 3/4 cups flour

1 egg white
1/2 cup finely chopped
  walnuts

Preheat the oven to 350 degrees.

Cream the margarine, brown sugar, sugar and cinnamon together in a large mixer bowl. Add the egg yolk; mix well. Add the flour gradually, beating well until thoroughly mixed. The dough will be thick and somewhat crumbly.

Press the mixture into a 9x13-inch baking pan.

Whisk the egg white until frothy. Brush on the top of the mixture. Sprinkle with the walnuts.

Bake at 350 degrees for 30 minutes. Cut into squares while hot. Let stand in the pan to cool.
—*Joan DeRose*

CUT-OUT COOKIES

36 cookies

The orange rind and butter give these cookies a unique and delicious flavor. Karen has spent many fun-filled afternoons during the holidays with her children decorating and baking these easy-to-make cookies.

1/2 cup butter, softened
1 cup sugar
1 egg, beaten
2 teaspoons grated
  orange rind
2 cups flour
1 teaspoon baking
  powder
1/2 teaspoon salt

Cream the butter in a mixer bowl. Add the sugar gradually, beating until light and fluffy. Stir in the egg and orange rind.

Sift the flour, baking powder and salt together. Add to the creamed mixture; mix well.

Shape the dough into a ball and wrap in waxed paper. Chill for 8 to 12 hours.

Preheat the oven to 325 degrees.

Roll the dough very thin on a lightly floured surface and cut with cookie cutters. Place on a cookie sheet.

Bake at 325 degrees for 8 to 10 minutes.

Cool on cookie sheet for 1 minute; remove to wire rack to cool completely.

May brush cookies with an egg white beaten with a small amount of water and sprinkle with colored sugars before baking. —*Karen Rich Douglas*

Insert wooden popsicle sticks into large sugar cookies before baking to make cookie-on-a-stick party favors or treats for children of all ages. Decorate the cookies to suit the occasion.

ELSIE'S PECAN SQUARES

24 squares

Marjorie is the granddaughter of George Hetzel, whose painting, Still Life with Concord Grapes and Apples (1897), *graces the cover of* Art in the Kitchen. *These chewy cookies with the firm edges are brownie-like in texture.*

1/2 cup butter
2 cups packed brown sugar
2 eggs, beaten
1 cup sifted flour
2 teaspoons baking powder
1 teaspoon vanilla extract
1 cup chopped pecans

Preheat the oven to 350 degrees.

Melt the butter in a medium saucepan. Stir in the brown sugar gradually, blending well. Spoon into a medium mixer bowl and let stand until cool.

Beat the eggs into the brown sugar mixture. Add the flour, baking powder and vanilla, beating until well blended.

Stir in the pecans. Spread the batter in a greased 9x13-inch metal baking pan.

Bake at 350 degrees for 35 minutes or until a wooden pick inserted in the center comes out clean.

Cut into squares while warm. Garnish with a sprinkling of confectioners' sugar. May add 3/4 cup chocolate chips with the pecans before baking.
—*Marjorie Hetzel*

If the dough for rolled cookies seems too soft, do not add more flour, as this will toughen the dough. Instead, chill it until it is firm and then roll a small amount at a time.

EMPIRE BISCUITS

30 cookies

This recipe was adapted from one found in an old Williamsburg book.

1¼ cups flour
⅓ cup sugar
1 teaspoon cinnamon
½ cup unsalted butter

5 tablespoons currant
   jelly
Vanilla Butter Icing
   (see below)

Preheat the oven to 350 degrees.

Sift the flour, sugar and cinnamon into a medium bowl. Cut the butter into the flour mixture with a pastry blender.

Knead gently on a lightly floured surface until the dough holds together; roll out very thin. Cut with a 1½-inch round cookie cutter. Place on a baking sheet.

Bake at 350 degrees for 10 to 12 minutes or until lightly browned. Cool on the cookie sheet for 1 minute; remove to a wire rack to cool completely.

Spread currant jelly on half the cookies. Top with the remaining cookies and press together gently.

Spread the Vanilla Butter Icing on top.

VANILLA BUTTER ICING

½ tablespoon unsalted
   butter, melted
½ cup confectioners'
   sugar
¼ teaspoon vanilla
   extract
1 tablespoon cream

Combine the butter, confectioners' sugar, vanilla and cream in a small bowl, blending until smooth.
—Joan DeRose

GINGER COOKIES

72 cookies

This tender cookie dough needs to be chilled or even frozen, then rolled or shaped in small amounts for easier handling.

3/4 cup shortening
1 cup sugar
1 egg
1/2 teaspoon cinnamon
1/2 teaspoon ground
    cloves
1 teaspoon ginger
1/4 cup molasses

2 1/2 cups flour
2 teaspoons baking soda

Cream the shortening and sugar in a mixer bowl until light and fluffy. Add the egg; mix well. Stir in the cinnamon, cloves and ginger. Add the molasses and blend well.

Sift the flour and baking soda together and add to the molasses mixture gradually, mixing until a soft dough forms.

Shape the dough into 2-inch diameter logs. Wrap each log in waxed paper and chill for 1 hour.

Preheat the oven to 375 degrees.

Cut the dough into 1/4-inch slices with a sharp knife and place on a nonstick cookie sheet.

Bake at 375 degrees for 6 minutes; do not overbake.

Cool on cookie sheet for 1 minute; remove to a wire rack to cool completely.
—*Margaret Brittingham*

KISS–ME COOKIES

60 cookies

Delicious, rich cookies sure to bring thank-you kisses for the baker.

1½ cups butter, softened
¾ cup sugar
1 tablespoon lemon
  extract
2¾ cups flour
1½ cups finely chopped
  blanched almonds

1 (14-ounce) package
  chocolate candy kisses
¼ cup confectioners'
  sugar

1 cup semisweet
  chocolate chips
1 tablespoon shortening

Cream the butter, sugar and lemon extract in a large mixer bowl until light and fluffy. Add the flour gradually, mixing well after each addition. Stir in the almonds.

Chill, covered, for 1 hour or longer.

Preheat the oven to 350 degrees.

Wrap 1 tablespoonful of dough around each candy kiss, covering the candy completely and shaping into a ball. Place the balls on ungreased cookie sheets.

Bake at 350 degrees for 8 to 12 minutes or until the bottom edges are golden brown. Let stand for 1 minute before removing to a wire rack to cool completely.

Sprinkle the cooled cookies lightly with the confectioners' sugar.

Melt the chocolate chips and the shortening in a small saucepan over low heat, stirring constantly until smooth. Drizzle the warm chocolate mixture over the top of the cookies. —*Karen Rich Douglas*

CRISPY DATE BALLS

50 cookies

Serve these at a holiday gathering.

1/2 cup butter, softened
1 cup sugar
1 egg, beaten
1 (8-ounce) package
dates, finely chopped
1 3/4 cups crisp rice cereal
1 cup finely chopped
walnuts
1/2 (7-ounce) package
flaked sweetened
coconut

Melt the butter in the top of a double boiler over hot water over low heat. Add the sugar, egg and dates. Cook for 8 to 10 minutes, stirring constantly. Let stand until slightly cooled.

Stir in the cereal and walnuts, mixing well.

Chill the mixture for 30 minutes.

Shape into balls about 1 inch in diameter. Roll the balls in the coconut. Place on waxed paper. Let stand until firm. —*Joan DeRose*

OATMEAL CRISPS

30 cookies

Make into giant cookies if you wish, but double the recipe if you do.

1/2 cup butter
3/4 cup sugar
2 tablespoons flour
1 teaspoon baking
powder
1 teaspoon cinnamon
1 egg
1 cup old-fashioned
rolled oats

Melt the butter in a medium saucepan. Remove from the heat; add the sugar, stirring until well blended.

Sift the flour, baking powder and cinnamon together. Add to the sugar mixture; mix well. Add the egg and oats, mixing well.

Drop by rounded teaspoonfuls 3 inches apart onto a buttered and floured cookie sheet.

Bake at 400 degrees for 8 to 10 minutes or until golden brown. Let stand on cookie sheet for 1 minute before removing to a wire rack to cool. —*Anne B. Robertshaw*

PITZELS

120 pitzels

Lamech, a member of the Westmoreland Museum staff, has been making pitzels for 20 years, and this is his own time-tested recipe. He says you must use the best grade of sugar. These delicious pitzels stay wonderfully crisp.

12 large eggs
3 cups sugar
1³/₄ cups Imperial
   margarine, melted
¹/₈ teaspoon salt
1 teaspoon vanilla extract
1 rounded tablespoon
   anise seeds
1 tablespoon baking
   powder
5¹/₂ cups flour

Preheat the pitzel iron.

Beat the eggs in a large mixer bowl. Add the sugar ¹/₂ cup at a time, mixing well after each addition. Add the cooled melted margarine, salt, vanilla and anise seeds. Sift the baking powder and flour together. Add to the egg mixture gradually, mixing well.

Drop the batter by teaspoonfuls onto the pitzel iron and bake until brown using manufacturer's instructions.

Wrap the pitzels in groups of 10 in plastic wrap to keep fresh. —*Lamech Long*

SAND TARTS

30 cookies

This is a very old recipe for a delicious cookie.

2 cups packed brown
   sugar
1 cup butter, softened
2 egg yolks
3 cups (or more) flour

1 egg white, lightly
   beaten
2 tablespoons sugar
2 tablespoons cinnamon
30 almond slivers

Preheat the oven to 350 degrees.

Cream the brown sugar and butter in a large mixer bowl. Blend the egg yolks into the brown sugar mixture. Add the flour ¹/₂ cup at a time, blending well after each addition.

Roll the dough very thin on a lightly floured surface. Cut with a round 2-inch cookie cutter and place on a nonstick baking sheet. Brush the tops lightly with the egg white and sprinkle with a mixture of sugar and cinnamon. Place 1 almond sliver in the center of each cookie.

Bake at 350 degrees for 15 minutes.
—*Regina Narad*

SCRUMPTIOUS BROWNIES

24 brownies

These brownies are a chocolate lover's dream.

8 (1-ounce) squares
  unsweetened baking
  chocolate
1 cup margarine

3 cups sugar
5 eggs
1½ cups flour

Preheat the oven to 350 degrees.

Melt the chocolate and margarine in a double boiler over hot water, blending well. Let stand until cool.

Combine the sugar and eggs in a large mixer bowl. Beat at high speed for 10 minutes.

Stir in the cooled chocolate mixture. Add the flour; mix well. Spread into a greased and floured 9x13-inch baking pan.

Bake at 350 degrees for 30 to 35 minutes or just until a knife inserted in the center comes out clean; do not overbake.

Let stand until cool. Cut into bars. —*Debbie Reese*

LEMON BARS DELUXE

30 bars

½ cup confectioners'
  sugar
2 cups flour
1 cup butter or
  margarine, softened

4 eggs, beaten
2 cups sugar
1 tablespoon grated
  lemon rind
⅓ cup lemon juice
¼ cup flour
½ teaspoon baking
  powder
Confectioners' sugar to
  taste

Sift ½ cup confectioners' sugar and 2 cups flour into a bowl; mix well. Cut in the butter until crumbly. Press into a 9x13-inch baking pan. Bake at 350 degrees for 20 minutes.

Combine the eggs, sugar, lemon rind and lemon juice in a bowl, beating until mixed. Add a sifted mixture of ¼ cup flour and baking powder; mix well. Spoon over the baked layer. Bake at 350 degrees for 20 to 25 minutes or until light brown. Sprinkle with confectioners' sugar. Cut into bars. —*Judith Morrow*

TOASTED WALNUT LACE COOKIES

50 cookies

For a delightful treat at your afternoon tea time, serve these delicious and delicate melt-in-your-mouth cookies.

1 cup old-fashioned
    rolled oats
1 cup sugar
1 cup toasted walnuts,
    finely chopped
1½ tablespoons flour
⅛ teaspoon baking
    powder

1 egg
½ cup unsalted butter,
    melted
½ teaspoon vanilla
    extract
½ teaspoon lemon
    extract
⅛ teaspoon almond
    extract

Preheat the oven to 350 degrees.

Line baking sheets with foil and spray with non-stick cooking spray.

Combine the oats, sugar, walnuts, flour and baking powder in a large bowl.

Beat the egg in a small mixer bowl until frothy. Stir in the cooled butter and the vanilla, lemon and almond flavorings; mix well. Add the egg mixture to the oats mixture, stirring until well mixed.

Drop by teaspoonfuls 3½ inches apart onto the prepared baking sheets.

Bake at 350 degrees for 10 to 12 minutes or until lightly browned.

Slide the foil from the baking sheets to a wire rack to cool completely. Peel the foil very gently away from each cookie.

These cookies freeze well but are delicate. Place waxed paper between the layers of cookies in a loaf pan and wrap for freezing. —*Eve Novak*

In all professions, without doubt but certainly in cooking, one is a student all his life. —Fernand Point (1897–1955), Restaurateur

LAUREL HIGHLANDS PUNCH

50 servings

1 quart fresh
    strawberries
2 (6-ounce) cans frozen
    orange juice
    concentrate
2 (6-ounce) cans frozen
    lemonade concentrate
8 (6-ounce) juice cans
    water
3 quarts ginger ale

Pour small amount of water into ring mold. Place some of the strawberries attractively in mold. Freeze long enough to set berries in place. Fill the remainder of the mold with water. Freeze until serving time.

Combine the orange juice and lemonade concentrates with the juice cans of water in a 2-gallon container; mix well. Chill until serving time.

Pour the punch as needed into a punch bowl. Add the ginger ale and the ice ring just before serving.
—*Art In The Kitchen Cookbook Committee*

TOY SHOW PUNCH

50 servings

Be sure to have ingredients to make twice as much punch as you expect to need. Adults love this refreshing drink, too.

2 (12-ounce) cans frozen
    pineapple juice
    concentrate, thawed
2 (12-ounce) cans frozen
    orange juice
    concentrate, thawed
2 (2-liter) bottles ginger
    ale
1/2 gallon orange sherbet

Combine the pineapple juice and orange juice concentrates in a large punch bowl.

Pour the ginger ale over the juice concentrates when ready to serve and stir until well mixed. Add scoops of the sherbet to the punch.
—*The Women's Committee*

SWEET SIGNATURES

SWEET SIGNATURES

Artists have not always signed their work; nor is there a consistent reason for either signing or not. Some 19th century American painters developed unique symbols or stylized signatures which were less disruptive to their final image yet still signaled their authorship. Whistler used a butterfly image; Blakelock encircled his with an arrowhead; Severin Roesen often incorporated his name into his paintings as an active element.

When an artist places his signature on his work, it signifies its completion and implies satisfaction. In a similar manner, the dessert at the end of the meal completes the menu, as sweetness tends to satisfy the palate. Savor the sweetness of the ending — the final flourish — the signature of the artist.

Severin Roesen (1815-1872)
Still Life with Fruit
Oil on Canvas, 36 x 50 inches
Gift of William A. Coulter Fund

BLUEBERRY SAUCE

6 servings

This recipe comes from the Cranberry Moose Restaurant in Yarmouth Port, Massachusetts. Blueberry sauce goes well on pancakes, French toast or ice cream. Orange juice gives this sauce a sensational flavor.

3/4 cup sugar
3/4 cup orange juice
1 pint blueberries
1 tablespoon fresh
   lemon juice

Dissolve the sugar in orange juice in a saucepan over low heat, stirring frequently. Add the blueberries.

Cook for 5 to 10 minutes or until of the desired consistency, stirring frequently. Stir in the lemon juice.

The sauce may be refrigerated for 2 to 3 weeks.
—*Jerry L. Finegold*

SUPER SIMPLE CHOCOLATE SAUCE

6 servings

1 cup sugar
2 tablespoons flour
1/4 cup baking cocoa
1/2 teaspoon salt
1 cup milk
1/4 cup butter
1 teaspoon vanilla extract

Combine the sugar, flour, baking cocoa and salt in a saucepan; mix well. Stir in the milk gradually.

Cook over low heat until the mixture thickens, stirring constantly.

Add the butter and vanilla; stir until well blended.
—*Mary "Sis" Herrington*

CHRISTMAS EGGNOG CHEESECAKE

10 servings

A red and green candied citron topping says "Merry Christmas." Serve small portions as it is quite rich.

1 (9-inch) graham
    cracker pie shell
1/2 teaspoon cinnamon

1 1/2 pounds cream
    cheese, softened
3/4 cup sugar
2 tablespoons brandy
1/4 cup dark rum
1 teaspoon vanilla extract
1/2 teaspoon ground
    nutmeg
3 large eggs

1 1/2 cups sour cream
1 1/2 tablespoons sugar
1/4 teaspoon vanilla
    extract
1/2 cup chopped green
    and red candied citron

Preheat the oven to 375 degrees.

Sprinkle the pie shell with cinnamon, pressing the cinnamon lightly into the shell.

Combine the cream cheese and the 3/4 cup sugar in a large mixer bowl and beat until smooth. Add the brandy, rum, 1 teaspoon vanilla and nutmeg; blend well. Add the eggs 1 at a time and beat just until blended.

Spoon the cream cheese mixture into the pie shell and spread evenly.

Bake at 375 degrees for 45 minutes or until puffed, light brown and softly set in the center. Remove from the oven and place on a wire rack to cool for 30 minutes.

Increase the oven temperature to 400 degrees.

Combine the sour cream, 1 1/2 tablespoons sugar and 1/4 teaspoon vanilla in a medium bowl and blend well.

Spoon the sour cream topping over the cream cheese mixture. Sprinkle the citron over the top.

Bake the cheesecake for 8 minutes or until the topping is firm. Place on a wire rack to cool.

Chill, covered, for 8 hours.

Sprinkle with additional cinnamon, nutmeg and a dash of rum before serving. —*Robert B. Weidlein*, **Huntland Farm Bed & Breakfast**

CARAMEL PECAN ICE CREAM CRÊPES

8 servings

Vary the ice cream filling and topping but prepare the crêpes in advance.

1 cup complete pancake
 mix
1 cup water
2 eggs
2 tablespoons superfine
 sugar

1 pint vanilla ice cream,
 softened
Caramel Sauce
 (see below)

Combine the pancake mix, water, eggs and sugar in a mixer bowl. Beat until the mixture is smooth. Let stand for 1 hour before cooking.

Heat an 8-inch nonstick skillet greased lightly with vegetable oil over low to medium heat. Spoon 2 tablespoons of the pancake batter into the heated skillet, tilting the skillet until the mixture coats the bottom.

Cook over low heat until the edges of the crêpe start to dry and bubbles appear in the center.

Turn the crêpe and brown the other side. Repeat the process until all the batter is used. Stack the finished crêpes between waxed paper strips and set aside.

Shape the softened ice cream into 6-inch logs. Wrap the logs with plastic wrap; place on a baking sheet and freeze for 2 hours or longer.

Roll the ice cream logs in the prepared crêpes and place seam side down in individual serving dishes.

Spoon the Caramel Sauce over each ice cream crêpe. Serve immediately.

CARAMEL SAUCE

1 cup packed brown
 sugar
1/4 cup butter
1/4 cup whipping cream
1/4 teaspoon rum extract
1/3 cup chopped pecans

Combine the brown sugar, butter and whipping cream in a saucepan; mix well.

Bring the mixture to a boil and reduce heat. Simmer for 2 1/2 minutes, stirring constantly. Remove from heat.

Add the rum extract and the pecans; mix well.
—*Sheila Quinn Smith*

CRANBERRY CRUMBLE

8 servings

Make a pretty presentation for this dessert by spooning the cranberry mixture with some golden brown topping into sherbet dishes and adding a dollop of whipped cream.

1 (12-ounce) package
  fresh cranberries
3/4 cup sugar
1/4 cup flour
3 medium pears

1/2 cup flour
1/4 cup packed brown
  sugar
1/4 cup sugar
2 tablespoons butter

Preheat the oven to 350 degrees.

Rinse the cranberries and drain well. Combine the cranberries with the sugar and flour in a saucepan. Cook over low heat until the sugar dissolves and the mixture begins to thicken, stirring constantly. Remove from the heat.

Peel and chop the pears. Add to the cranberry mixture and mix well.

Combine 1/2 cup flour, brown sugar, 1/4 cup sugar and butter in a medium bowl and mix until crumbly.

Pour the cranberry mixture into a buttered 9x9-inch baking dish. Top with the brown sugar topping. Bake at 350 degrees for 30 minutes.

Serve warm with freshly whipped cream or ice cream. —*Carol Vallozzi*

STRAWBERRIES ROMANOFF

4 servings

3 cups fresh strawberries
¼ cup light rum

1 envelope whipped
  topping mix
Cinnamon and nutmeg
  to taste

Rinse the strawberries and pat dry. Remove the stems carefully. Place the strawberries in a bowl and drizzle with the rum. Marinate the strawberries in the rum for 1 hour.

Prepare the whipped topping mix according to the package directions using skim milk. Fold in the cinnamon and nutmeg gently.

Alternate layers of the whipped topping and strawberries in dessert dishes. Garnish with mint leaves. —*Summer Friedlander*

SCOTCH CREAM

8 servings

Topped with gingersnaps, this special treat resembles a Scottish Bisque Tortoni. Originally, the ingredients for this dessert were blended into a health drink called "Athole Brose".

2 cups whipping cream
1 cup honey
½ cup Scotch whiskey

Beat the whipping cream in a mixer bowl until thick and stiff peaks form.

Combine the honey and whiskey in a separate bowl; whisk gently.

Fold the honey and whiskey into the whipped cream and blend well.

Spoon the mixture into individual freezer-safe dessert cups. Freeze for 2 hours. Serve frozen or slightly thawed. —*Vernie S. West*

SOUFFLÉ GLACÉ

12 servings

This "soufflé from heaven" is an elegant dessert that deserves to be paired with a very special dinner.

4 egg yolks
2 tablespoons water
1 tablespoon cognac
2 tablespoons sugar

2 egg whites
2 tablespoons sugar
1 tablespoon unflavored
  gelatin
6 tablespoons water
2 cups whipping cream
1 teaspoon grated
  orange rind
1/4 cup Grand Marnier
1 teaspoon vanilla extract
1/4 cup raspberry jam

1 tablespoon baking
  cocoa
1 tablespoon
  confectioners' sugar

Combine the egg yolks, 2 tablespoons of the water, the cognac and 2 tablespoons of the sugar in a double boiler; mix well. Simmer over hot water over low heat until the mixture thickens, beating constantly with a whisk. Remove from heat. Allow to cool.

Beat the egg whites and 2 tablespoons of the sugar in a bowl until stiff peaks form.

Soften the gelatin in the remaining water in a saucepan. Heat over low heat until dissolved.

Beat the whipping cream in a mixer bowl until thick. Add the grated orange rind, Grand Marnier and vanilla; mix well. Fold the egg yolk mixture and the gelatin into the whipped cream mixture gently. Fold in the egg whites gently.

Spoon a thin layer of raspberry jam into individual glass dessert dishes or a large shallow glass bowl. Top with the soufflé mixture. Chill for several hours to overnight.

Mix the baking cocoa with the confectioners' sugar. Sprinkle over the top just before serving.
—*Sue Jamison*

CHRISTMAS PORRIDGE

12 servings

This charming dish is usually served the night before Christmas Eve. The almond represents love, the apple represents health and the dime (in Swedish, 10 öre) represents richness for the next year. Santa Claus (Jultomten) would surely like a bowl set out on the porch for him the following night as well.

2 cups water
1 cup uncooked long
  grain rice
1 teaspoon salt
4½ cups milk
¼ cup whipping cream
1 tablespoon butter,
  softened
1 tablespoon sugar

1 toasted almond
1 small apple slice
1 silver dime,
  thoroughly cleaned

Cinnamon-sugar

Bring the water to a boil with salt in a medium saucepan. Stir in the rice. (Do not use instant rice.) Return to boiling; cook over low heat for 10 minutes.

Pour the milk into the rice mixture and simmer over low heat for about 30 minutes or until the porridge is thickened, stirring occasionally.

Add the whipping cream and butter, mixing until well blended.

Add the sugar, almond, apple slice and dime to the porridge; mix well.

Garnish each serving with a mixture of cinnamon and sugar. —*Karin E. Haile*

When folding beaten egg whites into another mixture, spoon ¼ of the beaten egg whites into the batter to lighten the mixture. Then add the remaining egg whites gently, but thoroughly folding them in.

ENGLISH SUMMER PUDDING

16 servings

This seasonal recipe is an English children's dessert of berries molded into bread. It looks like a steamed pudding but is served cold. It may be served in a very elegant fashion. The whipped cream complements the berries beautifully and is highly recommended, but may be omitted. The prepared pudding must be chilled for two days prior to serving time.

7 cups fresh raspberries
3 cups fresh blueberries
1 cup (or less) sugar
1 teaspoon cinnamon

20 slices (thinly-sliced) white bread

1 cup whipping cream
2 teaspoons confectioners' sugar
1/2 teaspoon vanilla extract
1 cup blueberries

Combine the raspberries and 3 cups of the blueberries with the sugar and cinnamon in a large bowl. Mix well, crushing some of the berries to extract the juices. Set aside.

Remove the crusts from the bread slices. Cut a large circular round from 1 slice of bread and place in the bottom of a 2-quart stainless steel bowl. Cut each of the remaining slices of bread into 2 trapezoidal pieces. Beginning at the bottom of the bowl, place the bread pieces attractively, overlapping slightly, to line the entire bowl. Repeat until the top layer extends over the edges of the bowl.

Fill the bread-lined bowl with the berry mixture, packing gently and forcing the juices into the bread. Fold the top layers of bread down over the berries; layer the remaining bread slices on top, covering the berries completely.

Cover the bowl with plastic wrap. Lay a plate slightly smaller than the rim of the bowl on top of the plastic wrap. Place a weight on the plate to force it down.

Chill for 2 days to allow the juices to soak into the bread.

Whip the whipping cream in a small bowl. Add the confectioners' sugar and vanilla, mixing until soft but pourable.

Remove the weight, plate and plastic wrap. Pour off most of the excess juice. Unmold onto a glass serving plate. Arrange the remaining 1 cup blueberries around the edge of the plate.

Slice and serve with the whipped cream drizzled over the top. —*Linda Austin*

STEAMED BLACK PUDDING

12 servings

Our traditional Christmas dinner dessert, the origins are lost, but it is believed to be an old English recipe. Serve after a fine dinner of standing rib roast and Yorkshire pudding or roasted goose. The aroma of this superb recipe brings back fond memories. Much easier to make than traditional plum pudding, it seems an appropriate addition to the Cratchet dinner table to serve to Ebenezer Scrooge and the Ghosts of Christmas Past, Present and Future.

1/2 cup pecans
1/2 cup raisins
1 1/2 cups flour
1 cup dark molasses
1 cup boiling water
1 teaspoon baking soda
1/2 teaspoon salt
1/2 teaspoon cinnamon
1/2 teaspoon grated
   nutmeg
1/2 teaspoon ground
   ginger
1/2 teaspoon ground
   cloves
1 egg, beaten

1 tablespoon butter,
   softened
1 teaspoon sugar
Brandy Hard Sauce
   (see below)

Coat the pecans and raisins with 2 tablespoons of the flour in a bowl; set aside.

Combine the molasses, boiling water and baking soda in a bowl, stirring until well blended. Mix the remaining flour with the salt, cinnamon, nutmeg, ginger and cloves. Add gradually to the molasses mixture, mixing well after each addition. Fold in the coated pecans and raisins. Add the egg, mixing well.

Butter a 6-cup mold and sprinkle with the sugar. Spoon the pudding mixture into the prepared mold.

Set the uncovered mold on the rack in a steamer. Add water to a depth of 1 inch. Cover and steam the pudding for 1 hour, checking the water level occasionally.

Serve warm with a very cold Brandy Hard Sauce. Garnish with a fresh holly sprig.

May prepare this recipe 1 to 2 days in advance. Reheats well wrapped in foil.

BRANDY HARD SAUCE

1/2 cup unsalted butter,
   softened
1 1/2 cups confectioners'
   sugar
1 tablespoon whipping
   cream
1 tablespoon brandy (or
   to taste)

Cream the butter in a small mixer bowl until soft. Stir in the confectioners' sugar, whipping cream and brandy by hand with wooden spoon.

Chill in the refrigerator. —*Jill Moore*

GATEAU CHOCOLATE MARIO

15 servings

This cake is so moist and delicious. It is particularly good when served with a chocolate glaze or with fresh fruit or whipped cream

10½ (1-inch) squares
   semisweet chocolate
7 ounces unsalted butter
⅛ teaspoon salt

1 teaspoon vanilla extract
8 egg yolks
1 cup plus 1 tablespoon
   sugar

8 egg whites
⅛ teaspoon cream of
   tartar

Melt the chocolate, butter and salt in a double boiler over hot water. Allow to cool

Add the vanilla to the chocolate mixture, blending well.

Combine the egg yolks and the sugar in a medium bowl. Beat until the mixture is slightly thickened and pale yellow in color. Add the chocolate mixture; blend well.

Beat the egg whites with the cream of tartar in a mixer bowl until stiff peaks form. Fold the stiffly beaten egg whites, ⅓ at a time, gently into the chocolate mixture.

Spoon the mixture into 2 greased 9-inch cake pans with removable bottoms.

Bake at 250 degrees for 2½ to 3 hours or until wooden pick inserted near center comes out clean. —*Jerry Finegold*

To make chocolate leaves for garnishing, wash fresh rose, lemon, camellia, gardenia or ivy leaves; pat dry. Melt 4 ounces sweet or semisweet chocolate in double boiler over hot water, stirring constantly. Brush melted chocolate on undersides of leaves with pastry brush. Place on waxed paper or foil-lined tray. Chill for 15 minutes or until firm. Peel leaves carefully from chocolate.

RED DEVIL'S FOOD CAKE

48 small servings

A cake that makes it worthwhile to break a diet. The recipe contributor notes that all who taste this cake "go crazy" and say this moist, rich cake is the best cake they've ever tasted.

2 cups sugar
2 cups flour, sifted
1/2 teaspoon salt
1 cup butter
1 cup water
4 tablespoons baking
  cocoa
2 eggs, beaten
1/2 cup buttermilk
1 teaspoon baking soda
1 teaspoon vanilla extract
1/2 ounce red food
  coloring
1 tablespoon white
  vinegar
Creamy Chocolate
  Frosting (see below)

Preheat the oven to 350 degrees.

Mix the sugar, flour and salt together.

Combine the butter, water and baking cocoa in a small saucepan. Bring to a rolling boil and remove from heat.

Combine the eggs, buttermilk, baking soda, vanilla, food coloring and vinegar in a medium mixer bowl. Beat until smooth. Add the flour mixture and the chocolate mixture alternately, beating well after each addition.

Pour the batter into a greased and floured 10x15-inch jelly roll pan. Bake at 350 degrees for 15 minutes or until the cake tests done.

Spread Creamy Chocolate Frosting over the top of the cake 5 minutes after removing from the oven.

The cake cuts best into neat squares if first refrigerated or frozen. Freeze for an hour or until the frosting is no longer sticky, cover with foil. Chill until serving time.

CREAMY CHOCOLATE FROSTING

1/2 cup butter
4 tablespoons baking
  cocoa
6 tablespoons milk
4 1/2 cups sifted
  confectioners' sugar
1 teaspoon vanilla extract
1/2 ounce red food
  coloring

Combine the butter, baking cocoa and milk in a saucepan. Bring to a full boil. Add the confectioners' sugar, vanilla and food coloring. Mix until smooth and creamy. —*Carol Ratner*

Rich Coconut Cake

16 servings

1 cup butter
1/2 cup shortening
3 cups sugar
6 eggs
3 cups flour
1/4 teaspoon salt
1 cup milk
1/2 teaspoon almond
  extract
1 teaspoon coconut
  flavoring
1 cup flaked coconut

Preheat the oven to 325 degrees.

Cream the butter, shortening and sugar in a medium bowl until light and fluffy. Add the eggs 1 at a time, mixing well after each addition.

Fold in the flour and salt alternately with the milk. Add the flavorings and blend well. Stir in the coconut.

Pour the batter into a greased and floured 12-cup bundt pan. Bake at 325 degrees for 1 1/4 to 1 1/2 hours or until a wooden pick inserted in the center of the cake comes out clean.

Cool in the pan for 15 minutes. Invert onto a wire rack to cool completely. Dust with confectioners' sugar. —*Cynthia Busch*

Blueberry Cake

16 servings

Like a cake of blueberry muffins!

2 cups blueberries
2 1/2 cups flour
1/2 cup butter, softened
1 1/2 cups sugar
2 eggs
2 teaspoons baking
  powder
1/8 teaspoon salt
1 cup milk
1 teaspoon vanilla extract

Preheat the oven to 350 degrees.

Toss the blueberries with a small amount of the flour and set aside.

Cream the butter and sugar in a mixer bowl until light and fluffy. Beat in the eggs. Add mixture of remaining flour, baking powder and salt with the milk and vanilla, mixing well.

Fold in the blueberries. Spoon into a greased and floured 12-cup bundt pan.

Bake at 350 degrees for 45 minutes or until cake tests done. Cool in the pan for 10 minutes. Invert onto a serving plate.

Dust with confectioners' sugar. —*Cynthia Bush*

'03 Kitchen Tour

EASY STRAWBERRY SHORTCAKE

12 servings

Easy to prepare ahead, easy to have the ingredients on hand, easy to assemble, and especially easy to eat!

1 pint vanilla ice cream

2 teaspoons superfine
    sugar
1 tablespoon light rum
1 pint fresh
    strawberries, hulled,
    sliced

1 cup whipping cream
1 tablespoon superfine
    sugar
1 tablespoon light rum
1 pound cake

Scoop the ice cream into balls and freeze for 2 hours or longer.

Combine 2 teaspoons sugar and 1 tablespoon rum in a medium bowl and mix well.

Cover the strawberries with the sugar and rum mixture and marinate for 3 to 8 hours.

Beat the whipping cream in a mixer bowl with 1 tablespoon sugar and 1 tablespoon rum until soft peaks form when the beaters are lifted. Do not overbeat.

Slice the pound cake.

Place the strawberries with a tablespoon of the rum marinade mixture on the pound cake slices on individual serving plates.

Top with the ice cream balls and serve with whipped cream. —*Sheila Quinn Smith*

Sprinkle fresh strawberries with some sugar. Pour over some orange juice, cover and refrigerate for a couple of hours. This makes for a refreshing dessert or is even lovely to serve at a brunch.

TANGY WHIPPED CREAM CAKE

12 servings

A recipe that "never fails," this rich cake may be prepared the day before serving.

1 (2-layer) package
    butter recipe golden
    cake mix
1/2 cup vegetable oil
4 eggs
1 (11-ounce) can
    mandarin oranges,
    undrained
Tangy Frosting
    (see below)

Preheat the oven to 375 degrees.

Combine the cake mix, oil, eggs and mandarin oranges in a medium mixer bowl. Beat at medium speed for 4 minutes. Pour the batter into 3 greased and floured 8-inch round cake pans.

Bake at 375 degrees for 20 to 25 minutes or until the cake tests done. Remove to a wire rack to cool.

Spread Tangy Frosting between the layers and over the top and side of the cake.

TANGY FROSTING

1 (20-ounce) can
    crushed pineapple,
    undrained, chilled
1 (4-ounce) package
    vanilla instant
    pudding mix
8 ounces whipped
    topping

Combine the pineapple, pudding mix and whipped topping in a bowl; mix well.

Chill for 30 minutes before frosting the cake.

The frosting may be made and chilled while the cake is baking. —*Helen Hartzell*

WHISKEY CAKE

16 servings

A wonderfully moist dessert cake with a slightly decadent taste—very nice to serve with fresh peaches. Must do the day before your party!

1 (2-layer) package
   white cake mix
1/2 cup vegetable oil
1 cup milk
4 eggs
1 (4-ounce) package
   vanilla instant
   pudding mix
2 tablespoons Canadian
   whiskey
1 cup chopped pecans
2 teaspoons flour

1/2 cup butter
3/4 cup sugar
3/4 cup whiskey

Preheat the oven to 325 degrees.

Combine the cake mix, oil, milk, eggs, pudding mix and whiskey in a medium mixer bowl; mix well.

Toss the pecans with the flour in a small bowl. Stir into the cake mixture. Spoon the batter into a greased and floured tube pan.

Bake at 325 degrees for 1 hour or until wooden pick inserted near center comes out clean.

Melt the butter in a saucepan over low heat; stir in the sugar. Add 3/4 cup whiskey and blend well.

Pour the whiskey topping over the hot cake in several stages for complete absorption. Let the cake cool in the pan for 2 hours. Remove the cake from the pan; wrap the cake in plastic wrap.

Chill the cake for 24 hours. Remove it from the refrigerator 1 hour before serving.
—*Catharine Celli*

BLITZ TORTE

8 servings

Originally from Milwaukee, Wisconsin, this recipe has been in the family for three generations.

1/2 cup butter, softened
1/2 cup superfine sugar
3 egg yolks
1/4 cup milk
1/2 teaspoon vanilla extract
1 cup cake flour
1 teaspoon baking powder
1/8 teaspoon salt

3 egg whites
1/2 teaspoon vanilla extract
1/2 cup sugar
1 (4-ounce) package almonds, chopped

Sour Cream Custard (see below)

Preheat the oven to 350 degrees.

Cream the butter and superfine sugar in a medium mixer bowl until light and fluffy.

Add the egg yolks 1 at a time, beating after each addition until the mixture is smooth. Add the milk and 1/2 teaspoon vanilla; mix well. Mix the cake flour, baking powder and salt together. Add to the egg mixture, mixing well.

Spoon the batter into 2 buttered and floured 8-inch round cake pans.

Beat the egg whites until soft peaks form. Stir in 1/2 teaspoon vanilla. Add 1/2 cup sugar gradually, beating until stiff peaks form. Spread over the batter in the cake pans. Sprinkle with the chopped almonds, pressing the almonds into the meringue.

Bake at 350 degrees for 30 minutes. Cool in the pans for 15 minutes. Remove to wire racks meringue side up to cool completely.

Place 1 cooled layer on a serving plate. Spread the Sour Cream Custard over the top. Top with the remaining layer.

SOUR CREAM CUSTARD

1 cup sour cream
1 egg
3 tablespoons sugar
1 teaspoon cornstarch

Scald the sour cream in a small saucepan.

Combine the scalded sour cream with the egg, sugar and cornstarch in the top of a double boiler over hot water.

Cook until the mixture is of a custard consistency, stirring constantly.

—Martha Oliver and Elizabeth Werner

SACHER TORTE

20 servings

Judith's mother was given this recipe in Austria when her father was teaching near Vienna on a Fulbright scholarship. She was seven years old and remembers the experience as an important time in her childhood.

6 (1-ounce) semisweet
  squares chocolate
1/2 cup sugar
1/2 cup butter
6 egg yolks
3/4 cup dry bread crumbs
1/4 cup finely ground
  blanched almonds
1/4 teaspoon salt
7 egg whites

1/2 cup apricot or
  raspberry jam
Chocolate Glaze
  (see below)

Preheat the oven to 325 degrees.

Grate the chocolate in a small bowl and set aside.

Cream the sugar and butter in a medium bowl.

Add the egg yolks 1 at a time, beating until light and fluffy.

Add the grated chocolate, bread crumbs, almonds and salt; mix well.

Beat the egg whites in a mixer bowl until stiff but not dry. Fold gently into the chocolate mixture.

Spoon the batter into a greased and floured 9-inch springform pan. Bake at 325 degrees for 30 to 45 minutes, or until the cake tests done. Let stand until slightly cool. Remove to wire rack to cool completely. Place on serving plate.

Cut the cooled cake into halves horizontally and spread the jam over the top of the bottom half. Place remaining half of cake on top. Pour the Chocolate Glaze over the top and side of the cake, smoothing with a spatula.

Chill for 3 hours or until the glaze hardens. Remove from the refrigerator 1/2 hour before serving. May serve with whipped cream.

CHOCOLATE GLAZE

3 tablespoons butter
3 tablespoons light corn
  syrup
1 tablespoon strong
  coffee
1 cup semisweet
  chocolate chips

Combine the butter, corn syrup and coffee in a medium saucepan; mix well. Cook over medium heat until the mixture begins to boil, stirring constantly. Remove from heat.

Add the chocolate chips to the butter mixture and stir until the chocolate chips melt. Let cool until of glaze consistency. —*Judith H. O'Toole*

TROPICAL SNOW

16 servings

A light dessert with a refreshing tart taste.

3 envelopes unflavored
  gelatin
1/4 cup cold water
1/4 cup lemon juice
2 cups canned grapefruit
  juice
3 1/2 cups canned
  pineapple juice
3/4 cup sugar
1/8 teaspoon salt
3 egg whites
Custard Sauce
  (see below)

Dissolve the gelatin in the cold water. Combine the gelatin and lemon juice in a double boiler. Heat over hot water until the gelatin dissolves, stirring constantly. Remove to a large bowl. Stir in the fruit juices, sugar and salt. Chill for 1 hour or until slightly set.

Beat the egg whites in a bowl until foamy. Add to the gelatin mixture, beating until foamy. Spoon into a serving dish.

Chill until completely set.

Serve in sherbet dishes with the Custard Sauce spooned over the top.

CUSTARD SAUCE

2 cups milk
1/2 cup sugar
3 egg yolks, beaten
1 1/2 teaspoons vanilla

Heat the milk and sugar in a saucepan over low heat. Bring almost to a boil.

Stir a small amount of the milk mixture into the egg yolks. Add the yolk mixture to the warm milk gradually, stirring constantly.

Cook over low heat until the mixture thickens slightly. Do not boil. Stir in the vanilla. Let stand until room temperature.

Serve over Tropical Snow. —*Beth Searfoss.*

TOASTED COCONUT CREAM PIE

8 servings

This is an easier and slightly less caloric version of a pie served at the Gourmet Dinner of April 1982.

¾ cup shredded coconut

1½ cups milk
1 (4-ounce) package
  vanilla pudding and
  pie filling mix
1 cup whipping cream

3 tablespoons apricot
  preserves
1 baked (9-inch) pie shell

Preheat the oven to 350 degrees.

Spread the coconut on a baking sheet. Bake for 7 to 10 minutes or until lightly browned, stirring occasionally to prevent burning. Cool slightly.

Combine the milk and pudding mix in a saucepan. Cook over medium-high heat until the mixture thickens and just begins to boil, stirring constantly.

Pour into a large bowl. Let cool, stirring occasionally to prevent lumping.

Whip the whipping cream until stiff peaks form. Fold gently into the pudding mixture.

Spread the preserves on the bottom of the pie shell. Spoon the pudding mixture evenly over the top of the preserves.

Sprinkle the toasted coconut over the top of pie. Chill for 4 hours before serving. —*Betty Hammer*

When making custard fillings, place plastic wrap over surface of custard while it is cooling to prevent a "skin" from forming.

PUMPKIN MALLOW PIE

8 servings

This pie may replace your own traditional pumpkin pie recipe. Great served with cinnamon-flavored coffee.

1 (16-ounce) can
   pumpkin
1 (10-ounce) package
   miniature
   marshmallows
1 teaspoon cinnamon
1/4 teaspoon salt

1 cup whipping cream
1 baked (9-inch) pie shell

1/2 cup whipping cream
1 teaspoon vanilla extract
1 tablespoon
   confectioners' sugar

Combine the pumpkin and marshmallows in a large heavy saucepan. Cook over low heat until well blended, stirring constantly. Cool. Place the saucepan over a basin filled with ice cubes. Beat until the mixture is ligh colored and until chilled. Add the cinnamon and salt, mixing well.

Whip 1 cup whipping cream in a bowl until thick but still pourable. Fold into the chilled pumpkin mixture. Pour into the pie shell, spreading evenly to form an attractive top.

Chill in the refrigerator.

Whip the remaining 1/2 cup whipping cream in a bowl until thick but still pourable. Add the vanilla and confectioners' sugar; mix well.

Pour 2 tablespoons of the whipping cream mixture over the center of each slice before serving.
—*Linda Austin*

CHESS PIE

6 servings

This is a fabulous version of the classic southern chess pie.

4 egg yolks
1 cup sugar
2 teaspoons cornmeal
1 teaspoon flour
1/4 teaspoon salt
1/2 cup melted butter,
   cooled
1 cup whipping cream,
   lightly whipped
1/2 teaspoon nutmeg
1 unbaked (9-inch) pie
   shell

Preheat the oven to 300 degrees.

Beat the egg yolks lightly in a medium mixer bowl. Add the sugar, cornmeal, flour, salt and butter, mixing well. Fold in the whipped cream; beat until smooth.

Sprinkle the nutmeg evenly in the pie shell; add the filling.

Bake at 300 degrees for 1 hour.

May use the leftover egg whites for meringue if desired. —*Shirley Wilcox*

MAPLE SUGAR PIE

6 to 8 servings

This is a sweet, delicious dessert for special occasions. Well worth the extra preparation time. The pie may be made up to 8 hours in advance of serving.

1½ cups plus 1
   tablespoon flour
2½ tablespoons sugar
½ teaspoon salt
½ cup plus 2
   tablespoons unsalted
   butter, chilled
4 tablespoons (or less)
   ice water

1 cup packed light
   brown sugar
3 tablespoons unsalted
   butter, softened
3 egg yolks
1 cup plus 3 tablespoons
   maple syrup
½ cup milk
3 egg whites

¾ cup whipping cream,
   chilled

Combine the flour, sugar and salt in a food processor container. Cut the chilled butter into pieces. Add to the flour mixture. Process until the mixture is coarse in texture. Add ice water 1 tablespoonful at a time, processing constantly until the dough holds together.

Shape the dough into a ball and flatten. Cover in plastic wrap. Chill for 30 minutes.

Preheat the oven to 375 degrees.

Roll the dough on a floured surface into a 13-inch round. Fit into a 10-inch pie plate, trimming and crimping the edge.

Beat the brown sugar, softened butter and egg yolks in a large mixer bowl until well blended. Add the maple syrup and milk, blending well.

Beat the egg whites in a medium mixer bowl until stiff but not dry peaks form; fold gently into the maple syrup mixture.

Spoon into the prepared pie plate.

Bake at 375 degrees for 1 hour or until the pie is browned around the edge and the filling is set. Cool to room temperature.

Beat the whipping cream in a medium mixer bowl until soft peaks form. Spoon the whipped cream into a decorator tube fitted with a medium star tip. Pipe decorative rosettes around the edge and middle of the pie. —*Isabel Haggerson*

Whipped cream rosettes may be piped onto waxed paper and stored, tightly covered, in the refrigerator until needed.

VSOP Pecan Pie

8 servings

VSOP is the abbreviation for "very superior old pale" pecan pie. The Cognac and whipping cream are the inspiration for this very rich and wonderful tasting pie that is a favorite during the Thanksgiving and Christmas holidays at the Austin home. May be prepared a day in advance.

3 eggs
1 cup sugar
1/2 teaspoon salt
2 tablespoons melted
   unsalted butter
1/2 cup dark corn syrup
1/2 cup whipping cream
2 tablespoons Cognac
1 teaspoon vanilla extract
1 cup pecan halves
1 unbaked (9-inch) pie
   shell, chilled

Preheat the oven to 375 degrees.

Beat the eggs, sugar, salt, butter, corn syrup and whipping cream in a large mixer bowl until creamy.

Add the Cognac and vanilla; mix well. Stir in the pecans.

Spoon the mixture into the chilled pie shell.

Bake at 375 degrees for 40 to 50 minutes or until the filling is set. Cool before serving.

—*Linda Austin*

Bake filled pie shells on the lowest rack since these need the hottest heat from underneath for baking properly.

BLUEBERRY TART

6 to 8 servings

Delicious served with coffee and shared with good friends.

2 cups fresh blueberries
1/4 cup sugar
2 tablespoons flour
Dash of cinnamon

1 cup flour
2 tablespoons sugar
1/2 cup butter, softened
1 tablespoon white
   vinegar

1 cup blueberries

Preheat the oven to 400 degrees.

Mix the 2 cups blueberries with 1/4 cup sugar, 2 tablespoons flour and cinnamon in a bowl. Set aside.

Combine the remaining 1 cup flour and 2 tablespoons sugar in a large mixer bowl.

Cut in the butter with a pastry blender; add the vinegar, blending until soft.

Spread the mixture on the bottom and 1 inch up the sides of an 8- or 9-inch springform pan. Add the prepared blueberry mixture.

Bake at 400 degrees for 1 hour or until the crust is golden brown. Remove to serving plate.

Sprinkle the remaining blueberries over the top. Serve warm. —*Andee Millstein*

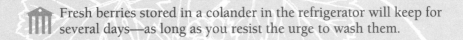 Fresh berries stored in a colander in the refrigerator will keep for several days—as long as you resist the urge to wash them.

FRESH SUMMER BERRY FRANGIPANE TART

10 servings

An outstanding presentation combined with delicious flavors.

Paté Brisée (see below)

½ cup unsalted butter, softened
⅓ cup plus 2 teaspoons sugar
1 teaspoon vanilla extract
2 large eggs
1 cup blanched slivered almonds, ground

1 (10-ounce) jar red currant jelly
1 tablespoon kirsch
2 cups fresh blueberries

Prepare the Paté Brisée.

Preheat the oven to 350 degrees.

Combine the ½ cup unsalted butter, sugar and vanilla in a medium mixer bowl. Add the eggs; mix well. Stir in the almonds and mix well. Spread the frangipane in the prepared pastry shell.

Bake at 350 degrees for 40 minutes or until set. Cool.

Melt the currant jelly in a small saucepan over low heat. Add the kirsch. Bring to a boil, stirring constantly; reduce heat. Simmer for 1 minute.

Brush the glaze over the top of the cooled tart.

Arrange the blueberries in a decorative pattern on the tart. May substitute strawberries or raspberries for the blueberries, or use a combination.
—*Linda Earnest,* **The Earnest Gourmet**

PATÉ BRISÉE

1¼ cups flour
¼ teaspoon salt
6 tablespoons chilled unsalted butter
2 tablespoons cold vegetable shortening
3 tablespoons ice water

Combine the flour and salt in a medium bowl. Cut in the 6 tablespoons butter and shortening with a pastry blender until the mixture resembles cornmeal. Add the ice water and mix until a dough forms.

Shape into a ball. Roll ⅛ inch thick on a floured surface. Fit into an 11-inch round tart pan with a removable fluted rim. Prick the pastry with a fork. Chill for 30 minutes.

GALLERY GUIDE

We have brought art into your kitchen with a cookbook that offers — along with kitchen-tested recipes and suggestions as to their artistic presentation in the menu and on the table — a taste of art history and a sampling of the museum's outstanding collection. For the casual visitor or serious student, a gallery guide is an important aid in planning and enjoying a museum trip. It locates by map or description the physical location of galleries and the works displayed there and provides specifics about museum hours and times and dates of exhibitions. The guide may be as brief as a labeled one-page floor plan or the size of book with great detail, going beyond gallery information, to include all the ingredients that comprise a vital museum.

In much the same way, we include a guide to our cookbook. It will help you find the particular recipe you want, the nutritional analysis of that recipe, or a substitution that will be helpful to you. You will also find the final and most important ingredient to *Art in the Kitchen* — an acknowledgement of all those people who helped to make our cookbook a reality!

Henry Lee McFee (1886-1953)
Interior with Still Life, 1931
Oil on Canvas, 46 x 40 inches
Gift of Dr. and Mrs. John J. McDonough

COOKBOOK COMMITTEE

Co-Chairs: Linda Austin, Jill Cook, Joan DeRose, Sue Jamison
Advisors: Judith H. O'Toole, Director; Dr. Paul A. Chew, Director Emeritus

Committee:

Linda Austin	Sue Jamison
Joan Beidler	Rose Mack
Susan Bowman	Tracy Morford
Catharine Celli	Judith Morrow
Mario Celli	Judith H. O'Toole
Paul A. Chew	Phyllis Pack
Jill Cook	Sue Pollins
Joan DeRose	Debbie Reese
Karen Douglas	Melissa Rodgers
Summer Friedlander	Libbett Weidlein
Virginia Grosscup	Robert Weidlein
Isabel Haggerson	Vernie West
Claudia Harbaugh	Lee Wood
Nancy Jamison	

The Cookbook Committee thanks the staff of the
Westmoreland Museum of Art for their generous support
and assistance, particularly Janet Carns, Eugene Komives,
Sara Jane Lowry, Regina Narad, Clara Pascoe and Audrey Wright.

CONTRIBUTORS

We would like to express our gratitude to the following people for their generous time and efforts given to *Art in the Kitchen*—the contributors, evaluators, testers, and tasters, and especially the gracious hosts of the tasting parties.

George Austin
Linda Austin
Charlotte Bailey
Joan Beidler
Linda Beidler
Win Beidler
Sue Birmingham
Louise Rahl Bolling
Vicki Booher
Susan Bowman
Colette Brewster
Margaret Brittingham
Elaine Bryan
Cynthia Busch
Susan Butz
Phyllis Caplan
Catharine Celli
Mario Celli
Paul A. Chew
Barbara L. Childs
Kathryn Chillingworth
Nancy Clarke
Patricia Clawson
Sandy Cole
Sarah Collins
Dorothy Cook
James Cook
Jeanne M. Cook
Jill Cook
Ruth Cook
Lucia Coulter
Hadley Herrington Debevoise
Heidi Herrington Debevoise
Joan DeRose
Johny DeRose
P. Louis DeRose
Karen Rich Douglas
Linda Earnest
Juliette Epstein

Jerry Finegold
Summer Friedlander
Marilyn Gaut
Bud Gibbons
Cicely Gilbert
Margie Gray
Greensburg Country Club
Virginia Grosscup
Aaronel deRoy Gruber
Isabel Haggerson
Karin E. Haile
Dee Hamilton
Betty Hammer
Claudia Harbaugh
Helen F. Hartzell
Sande Hendricks
Becky Henry
Sarah Henry
Mary Herrington
Marjorie Hetzel
Annette Hitchman
Ann S. Holmes
Rebecca Humphrey
Barbara Jamison
Elizabeth T.E. Jamison
Kathryn Jamison
Margaret Jamison
Nancy B. Jamison
Sue Jamison
Diana Jannetta
Irene S. Johnson
Dorothea Kaufmann
Pat Kelley
Debra King
Irene Klingensmith
Gene Komives
Reta S. Kuyat
Alice S. Laurich
Marge Lentz

Sondra Lettrich
JoAnn Lightcap
Lamech Long
Charles H. Loughran
Isabelle D. Lynch
Sally Loughran
Ann M. Macdonald
Caroline T. Mack
Rose Mack
Suzanne MacLennan
Mary Todd Marchand
Marilee Grosscup Matteson
Helen Matzie
Mary Ann McGuigan
Alice McKenna
Michaelene V. McWhinney
Helen Miller
Megan Cole Miller
Richard A. Miller
Andee Millstein
Joe Mitinger
Lisa Moeller
Jill Moore
Anne Morford
Dick Morford
Tracy Morford
Judith Morrow
Regina Narad
Eve Novak
Judith H. O'Toole
Martha Oliver
Arnie Palmer
Winnie Palmer
Clara Pascoe
Margot Perot
Ross Perot
Barbara Pierce
Mae Pierce
Berenice Pittler

Sue Pollins
Martha Raak
Annette Rathbun
Carol Ratner
Debbie Reese
Anne Robertshaw
Elizabeth Rodgers
Melissa Rodgers
Beth Searfoss
Eleanor Smith
Marquis M. Smith, III
Sheila Q. Smith
Stella Smith
Doris Springer
Mary Squilla
Rudy Stanish
Madge Steel
Amy Stern
Audrey Stern
Doris Stillman
Lila Swartz
Dee Thomas
Geraldine Trumbetta
Jackie Tumulty
Edie Valdemi
Carol Vallozzi
Ernie Vallozzi
Robert A. Walsh
Gladys Waugaman
Libbet Weidlein
Robert Weidlein
Elizabeth Werner
Vernie S. West
Jean Wilcox
Shirley Willcox
Sheryl K. Wolf
Women's Committee
Lee Wood
Sophie H. Zamborsky

NUTRITIONAL PROFILE GUIDELINES

The editors have attempted to present these family recipes in a form that allows approximate nutritional values to be computed. Persons with dietary or health problems or whose diets require close monitoring should not rely solely on the nutritional information provided. They should consult their physicians or a registered dietitian for specific information.

Abbreviations for Nutritional Profile

Cal — Calories	Fiber — Dietary Fiber	Sod — Sodium
Prot — Protein	T Fat — Total Fat	g — grams
Carbo — Carbohydrates	Chol — Cholesterol	mg — milligrams

Nutritional information for these recipes is computed from information derived from many sources, including materials supplied by the United States Department of Agriculture, computer databanks, and journals in which the information is assumed to be in the public domain. However, many specialty items, new products, and processed foods may not be available from these sources or may vary from the average values used in these profiles. More information on new and/or specific products may be obtained by reading the nutrient labels. Unless otherwise specified, the nutritional profile of these recipes is based on all measurements being level.

- **Artificial sweeteners** vary in use and strength so should be used "to taste," using the recipe ingredients as a guideline. Sweeteners using aspartame (NutraSweet and Equal) should not be used as a sweetener in recipes involving prolonged heating, which reduces the sweet taste. For further information on the use of these sweeteners, refer to package.
- **Alcoholic ingredients** have been analyzed for the basic ingredients, although cooking causes the evaporation of alcohol, thus decreasing caloric content.
- **Buttermilk, sour cream**, and **yogurt** are the types available commercially.
- **Cake mixes** which are prepared using package directions include 3 eggs and ½ cup oil.
- **Chicken**, cooked for boning and chopping, has been roasted; this method yields the lowest caloric values.
- **Cottage cheese** is cream-style with 4.2% creaming mixture. Dry curd cottage cheese has no creaming mixture.
- **Eggs** are all large. To avoid raw eggs that may carry salmonella, as in eggnog or 6-week muffin batter, use an equivalent amount of commercial egg substitute.
- **Flour** is unsifted all-purpose flour.
- **Garnishes**, serving suggestions, and other optional additions and variations are not included in the profile.
- **Margarine** and **butter** are regular, not whipped or presoftened.
- **Milk** is whole milk, 3.5% butterfat. Lowfat milk is 1% butterfat. Evaporated milk is whole milk with 60% of the water removed.
- **Oil** is any type of vegetable cooking oil. **Shortening** is hydrogenated vegetable shortening.
- **Salt** and other ingredients to taste as noted in the ingredients have not been included in the nutritional profile.
- If a choice of ingredients has been given, the nutritional profile reflects the first option. If a choice of amounts has been given, the nutritional profile reflects the greater amount.

Pg #	Recipe Title (Approx Per Serving)	Cal	Prot (g)	Carbo (g)	T Fat (g)	% Cal from Fat	Chol (mg)	Fiber (g)	Sod (mg)
11	Della Robbia Brie[1]	181	6	25	7	35	25	3	163
12	Pâté Emeritus	81	8	1	4	48	59	<1	260
13	May Wine Punch	69	<1	2	<1	<1	0	<1	4
13	Women's Committee Chicken Salad	454	24	10	36	71	81	3	355
14	Chicken Salad Sandwich Loaf	646	26	33	46	64	120	3	835
15	Dr. Chew's Creamy Pea Soup	180	9	18	8	41	25	6	482
15	Basil Cherry Tomatoes	44	1	3	4	70	9	1	41
16	The Plain Basic Omelet	325	19	2	27	74	667	0	839
17	The Party Ham	425	57	15	13	29	125	<1	3173
17	Ham Slice with Potatoes	328	39	13	13	35	95	1	1941
18	Roast Rack of Lamb	208	23	3	11	50	74	1	82
18	Garlic-Mustard Glaze for Lamb	44	1	1	4	88	0	<1	200
19	Lucia's Lamb Stew	356	21	25	19	49	88	3	348
20	Banana Cake	276	4	44	10	32	36	1	214
21	Poor Man's Cakes 1892	370	4	74	7	17	0	2	169
22	Cocoa Bavarian Note	479	11	53	27	49	138	2	151
23	Chocolate Charlotte	232	4	20	16	61	124	1	40
24	Frozen Pudding	351	4	31	24	60	112	<1	48
25	Montrose Sauce	210	2	4	20	83	119	0	23
25	Melba Sauce	72	<1	19	<1	1	0	3	1
26	Royal Lemon Custard Meringue	288	4	40	14	42	157	<1	46
29	Barbecued Water Chestnuts	65	1	5	5	63	5	<1	108
30	Preview Night Cheese Squares	108	2	6	8	70	10	1	152
30	Cocktail Swirls	54	1	4	4	64	9	0	111
31	Peanut Butter and Bacon Squares	65	2	4	5	68	4	<1	107
31	Pinwheel Hors d'Oeuvre	39	1	3	3	62	5	<1	88
32	Marsala Mushrooms	82	1	6	4	38	4	1	135
33	Miniature Reubens	166	7	6	13	70	24	1	463
34	Herbed Zucchini Squares	52	2	4	4	56	1	<1	90
35	Artichoke Cheese Spread	81	2	1	8	86	12	0	118
35	Bleu Cheese Lovers' Delight	132	5	1	12	81	35	0	319
36	Caponata	72	2	7	5	57	0	2	256
37	Hot Crab Dip	57	3	1	5	75	17	<1	74
37	Java Nut Brie	185	7	6	14	68	33	<1	209
38	Curried Shrimp Dip	64	3	1	5	77	39	<1	60
38	Smokey Appetizer Pâté	66	4	1	5	72	24	<1	123
39	Perky Tex-Mex Dip	164	6	11	11	59	22	3	802
40	Seafood Salsa with Chips	36	4	4	<1	15	10	<1	78
41	Widower's Hors d'Oeuvre	87	1	1	9	91	33	0	13

Pg #	Recipe Title (Approx Per Serving)	Cal	Prot (g)	Carbo (g)	T Fat (g)	% Cal from Fat	Chol (mg)	Fiber (g)	Sod (mg)
41	Curry Dip for Vegetables	170	<1	1	19	96	16	<1	298
42	Chinese Fried Walnuts[2]	46	1	3	4	71	0	<1	1
43	Sugar-and-Spice Pecans	58	1	4	5	67	0	<1	52
43	Power Punch	240	<1	14	<1	<1	0	<1	15
44	Champagne Punch	165	<1	22	<1	<1	0	<1	10
44	Ruby Punch	159	1	40	<1	1	0	1	13
47	Spinach and Sun-Dried Tomato Calzone	153	8	13	8	45	20	1	343
48	Queen Anne Cucumber Sandwiches	48	1	4	3	59	9	<1	102
48	Hot Ham and Cheese Sandwiches	259	10	28	12	41	68	1	905
49	Red Pepper and Spinach Bisques	298	12	15	22	64	69	4	1297
50	Avgolémono	83	6	8	3	30	71	<1	539
51	Chicken Salad with Curry Dressing	464	24	22	33	64	85	5	230
52	R.B.'s Chicken Salad	448	26	18	31	61	102	1	349
53	Elegant Garden Pasta Salad	464	25	45	21	40	119	5	779
54	Horseradish and Tomato Aspic	67	2	16	<1	1	0	1	447
54	Salmon and Dill Mold	200	10	2	17	76	65	<1	142
55	Tomato and Raspberry Mold	92	1	12	5	45	5	<1	118
56	Chicken and Lemon Mousse	328	26	17	18	49	114	1	575
57	Shrimp Mousse	166	7	3	14	77	64	<1	267
58	Tuna Mousse	204	6	2	20	85	61	<1	397
59	Zesty Mandarin Orange Salad[3]	49	1	12	<1	4	0	1	29
59	Walnut Dressing	569	2	37	48	73	8	1	299
59	Almond Dressing	177	0	4	18	90	0	0	89
60	Monet's Garden Salad	140	1	4	14	85	0	1	96
61	Spinach and Bacon Salad	365	12	8	34	79	12	4	634
62	Woodland Wedding Salad	186	5	16	12	58	12	3	150
63	Balsamic Dressing	49	<1	<1	5	98	0	0	6
63	Celery Seed Dressing	75	<1	7	6	64	0	<1	107
64	Raspberry Vinaigrette Dressing	11	<1	1	1	76	0	<1	<1
64	Rose Vinegar	Nutritional information for this recipe is not available.							
65	Steak and Eggs Benedict	564	53	14	31	51	419	1	329
66	Grilled Shrimp with Rice	232	19	35	2	9	142	1	832
66	Chiles Rellenos Casserole	437	28	10	32	66	198	1	1607
67	Savory Mushroom Pie	294	6	8	28	85	162	2	848
68	Real Man's Quiche	650	26	29	48	66	292	1	755
69	Herbed Cheese Strudel	397	10	15	34	75	146	1	339
70	Cranberry Coffee Cake	368	4	48	19	45	35	2	384
71	Carrot Bread	226	3	32	10	39	27	1	87
72	Blueberry Bliss Muffins	163	3	25	6	33	38	1	160

Pg #	Recipe Title (Approx Per Serving)	Cal	Prot (g)	Carbo (g)	T Fat (g)	% Cal from Fat	Chol (mg)	Fiber (g)	Sod (mg)
73	Raspberry Streusel Muffins	328	5	41	17	45	60	2	334
74	Zucchini and Basil Muffins	168	2	16	11	57	29	<1	88
75	Easy Cold-Oven Popovers	80	3	9	4	40	43	<1	65
76	French Toast à la Orange	217	6	28	9	38	122	1	233
77	Very Light and Excellent Waffles	429	11	35	27	58	136	1	276
78	Celebration Bread Pudding	370	8	47	17	42	172	1	276
81	Zesty Hummus Dip	137	4	13	8	52	0	1	136
81	Fruited Mint Tea	113	<1	29	<1	1	0	<1	3
82	Bloody Mary Mix	26	1	6	<1	3	0	1	662
82	Corn and Chicken Soup[4]	302	29	8	17	52	72	2	288
83	Cold Cucumber Soup	210	8	17	14	55	30	3	168
84	Spicy Gazpacho	59	2	13	1	8	0	3	458
85	Bok Choy Salad	344	4	19	30	75	0	2	380
86	Black Bean Salad	250	11	37	8	31	0	7	729
87	Couscous and Sun-Dried Tomatoes	153	4	18	7	43	0	1	243
88	French River Cucumber Salad	84	2	6	6	63	13	1	151
88	Green Beans Sebastian	320	5	19	27	73	0	8	148
89	Red Potato Salad with Grilled Scallions	172	3	32	4	22	5	3	114
90	Quinoa Salad	576	19	80	22	33	0	2	543
90	Flank Steak Nova Scotia	337	20	25	19	48	76	2	942
91	Grilled Leg of Lamb	459	39	5	31	61	121	1	240
92	Grilled Breast of Chicken	157	26	1	5	28	72	<1	63
93	Tomato Cheese Tart	305	10	24	19	56	24	2	572
94	Lemon Poppy Seed Pound Cake	227	4	31	10	39	75	1	117
95	Chocolate Lover's Pecan Brownies	213	2	25	13	52	37	2	62
95	Potato Chip Cookies	192	3	16	14	63	21	1	94
96	Luscious Linzer Tart	726	10	94	36	43	98	4	264
99	French Market Soup	188	13	23	6	26	10	8	537
100	Cabbage Soup	47	3	7	1	21	5	1	245
100	Leek and Potato Soup	311	13	30	16	45	49	4	984
101	Eggplant Salad Romanian-Style	167	2	11	14	71	0	4	6
102	Lemon Potato Salad	412	3	23	36	75	26	3	501
102	Sherried Pot Roast	313	36	4	15	44	118	<1	766
103	Tournedos Rossini[5]	546	47	18	28	47	162	1	381
103	Beef Barley Vegetable Stew	301	27	30	8	23	47	9	1079
104	Sugar Hill Meat Loaf	422	29	21	24	52	168	1	584
104	Ham Loaves	528	49	48	15	26	183	1	1434
105	Herbed Pork Tenderloins	318	20	<1	21	59	56	0	41
105	Veal Scaloppine with Marsala	484	21	9	37	68	110	<1	173

Pg #	Recipe Title (Approx Per Serving)	Cal	Prot (g)	Carbo (g)	T Fat (g)	% Cal from Fat	Chol (mg)	Fiber (g)	Sod (mg)
106	Chicken Almond Casserole	413	27	14	28	60	99	1	1168
106	Brandied Peaches	171	1	29	<1	1	0	1	9
107	Chicken Chili	496	48	34	18	33	108	7	698
108	Currant Breast of Chicken	250	27	29	3	11	72	<1	104
108	Chicken Mirabelle	285	27	20	10	33	72	2	290
109	Pollo al Parmigiana	458	39	6	28	56	139	1	901
110	Rolled Chicken Fillets	1111	56	37	83	65	192	6	943
111	Chicken Saltimbocca	383	34	10	21	49	130	1	422
112	Roast Long Island Duck	1175	56	54	80	61	237	3	318
113	Chicken with Charred Hot Peppers	333	22	18	20	52	43	4	1215
114	Chicken Curry[6]	1025	41	110	54	45	83	15	1289
116	Cajun Crab Cakes[7]	343	28	10	19	50	261	1	519
117	Baked Lobster Tails	308	38	6	12	38	162	<1	976
117	Tarragon Orange Roughy	160	18	5	8	44	24	1	75
118	Salmon Tango	467	34	16	28	55	105	<1	607
118	La Costa Salmon	248	26	5	14	49	79	1	66
119	Grilled Shrimp with Prosciutto	563	35	2	43	68	120	<1	1706
119	Mediterranean Shrimp	221	20	6	9	35	177	2	561
120	Super Seafood Casserole	241	16	8	15	57	125	1	355
121	Spaghetti Carbonara	399	17	54	12	28	175	2	280
122	Dr. Chew's Puttanesca Sauce	812	25	125	24	27	12	9	1051
123	Linguini Marinara	321	9	55	8	22	0	4	424
123	Tomato-Tomato Sauce	187	1	6	18	85	0	2	265
124	Asparagus à la Orange	34	3	7	<1	6	0	2	3
124	Creamed Asparagus in Pastry Shells	353	8	25	26	64	25	2	547
125	Best-Ever Beets	369	6	31	25	60	57	3	635
126	Nutted Broccoli with Poppy Seeds	257	5	10	23	77	36	2	171
126	Marinated Broccoli[8]	164	2	4	17	86	0	2	867
127	Eggplant Tian	135	6	18	5	33	7	7	269
128	Peas with Cucumber	55	4	10	<1	5	<1	4	295
128	New Potatoes à la Smitone	190	6	20	10	47	22	2	1297
129	Steamed New Potatoes with Garlic	134	3	31	<1	1	0	3	10
129	Spaghetti Squash Parmesan	212	6	11	16	68	46	1	589
130	Candied Sweet Potatoes	319	2	67	6	16	16	3	78
130	Tomato Pudding	232	2	31	12	45	0	1	403
131	Stir-Fried Vegetables	129	5	14	7	45	0	4	323
132	Cranberry Salsa	100	<1	26	<1	1	0	2	2
132	Pineapple Salsa	20	<1	5	<1	7	0	1	1
133	Pineapple Gratin	124	1	23	3	24	49	<1	37

Pg #	Recipe Title (Approx Per Serving)	Cal	Prot (g)	Carbo (g)	T Fat (g)	% Cal from Fat	Chol (mg)	Fiber (g)	Sod (mg)
133	Mushrooms Florentine	271	2	4	17	86	0	2	867
134	Easy Mushroom Sauce	231	2	5	23	86	72	1	265
134	Mushroom and Wild Rice Casserole	273	6	29	16	50	41	1	1018
135	Wild Rice and Apricot Stuffing	404	15	60	13	28	16	4	1012
135	Savory Herbed Rice	200	4	30	6	30	16	<1	294
136	Arnie's Spoon Bread	287	9	26	17	52	98	2	625
136	Parsnip Purée	142	2	18	8	50	21	4	66
137	Sweet and Spicy Mustard Ring	74	2	7	5	56	49	0	37
137	Cucumber and Honey	284	1	76	<1	0	0	1	6
138	Fresh Basil Pesto	386	8	2	40	87	29	<1	538
141	Almond Macaroons	49	1	8	2	29	0	1	4
142	Barbie™-Has-My-Heart Cookies	144	2	15	9	56	9	1	67
143	Black Walnut Refrigerator Cookies	99	1	13	5	44	19	<1	106
144	Blondies	199	3	27	10	43	44	1	128
145	Decadent Brown Sugar Squares	271	3	32	15	49	56	1	156
146	Chocolate Nut Wafers	52	1	5	3	57	11	<1	27
146	Cinnamon Squares	76	1	8	5	55	4	<1	47
147	Cut-Out Cookies	118	1	11	8	61	20	<1	120
148	Elsie's Pecan Squares	147	2	19	7	44	28	<1	78
149	Empire Biscuits	73	1	10	3	41	9	<1	2
150	Ginger Cookies	50	1	7	2	41	3	<1	24
151	Kiss-Me Cookies	143	2	14	10	58	14	1	53
152	Crispy Date Balls	74	1	9	4	48	9	1	33
152	Oatmeal Crisps	61	1	7	3	49	15	<1	45
153	Pitzels	72	1	10	3	40	21	<1	46
153	Sand Tarts	153	2	22	7	38	31	1	70
154	Scrumptious Brownies	258	3	34	14	46	44	2	104
154	Lemon Bars Deluxe	159	2	23	7	39	45	<1	77
155	Toasted Walnut Lace Cookies	56	1	6	4	56	9	<1	3
156	Laurel Highlands Punch	46	<1	12	<1	1	0	<1	5
156	Toy Show Punch	114	1	27	1	5	2	<1	20
159	Blueberry Sauce	138	1	35	<1	2	0	1	3
159	Super Simple Chocolate Sauce	239	2	39	10	34	26	1	277
160	Christmas Eggnog Cheesecake	614	9	51	41	58	154	1	456
161	Caramel Pecan Ice Cream Crêpes	361	5	47	18	43	98	1	337
162	Cranberry Crumble	244	2	54	3	12	8	4	32
163	Strawberries Romanoff	230	6	25	9	35	2	3	90
163	Scotch Cream	366	1	37	22	52	82	0	24
164	Soufflé Glacé	211	3	11	17	69	125	<1	30

Pg #	Recipe Title (Approx Per Serving)	Cal	Prot (g)	Carbo (g)	T Fat (g)	% Cal from Fat	Chol (mg)	Fiber (g)	Sod (mg)
165	Christmas Porridge	143	4	18	6	38	22	<1	235
166	English Summer Pudding	244	4	43	7	25	21	4	187
167	Steamed Black Pudding	354	4	54	15	38	43	2	186
168	Gateau Chocolate Mario	280	5	20	23	67	138	3	38
169	Red Devil's Food Cake	146	1	22	6	37	25	<1	105
170	Rich Coconut Cake	596	7	78	29	44	150	2	245
170	Blueberry Cake	224	3	37	7	28	44	1	117
171	Easy Strawberry Shortcake	245	3	23	16	56	101	1	140
172	Tangy Whipped Cream Cake	421	5	58	20	41	71	<1	147
173	Whiskey Cake	413	4	42	23	49	71	1	383
174	Blitz Torte	455	8	43	29	57	151	2	288
175	Sacher Torte	242	4	27	15	52	80	2	154
176	Tropical Snow	144	4	28	2	13	44	<1	30
177	Toasted Coconut Cream Pie	340	4	30	24	61	47	2	262
178	Pumpkin Mallow Pie	408	4	46	25	53	61	2	225
178	Chess Pie	604	5	50	44	64	237	1	428
179	Maple Sugar Pie	792	8	104	40	44	217	1	251
180	VSOP Pecan Pie	476	5	54	27	50	108	1	317
181	Blueberry Tart	310	3	41	16	45	41	2	161
182	Fresh Summer Berry Frangipane Tart	514	8	49	34	57	86	4	82

[1]Nutritional profile does not include Fruit-Fresh.
[2]Nutritional profile does not include oil for frying.
[3]Nutritional profile does not include dressing.
[4]Nutritional profile does not include cream-style corn soup.
[5]Nutritional profile does not include foie gras.
[6]Nutritional profile does not include Curry Condiments on page 115.
[7]Nutritional profile does not include butter or oil for frying.
[8]Nutritional profile includes entire amount of marinade.

ORDER INFORMATION

Art in the Kitchen
Westmoreland Museum of Art
221 North Main Street
Greensburg, Pennsylvania 15601
Phone: (412) 837-1500   Fax: (412) 837-2921

Please send _____ copies of *Art in the Kitchen* @ 17.95 each   _____
Pennsylvania residents add 6% sales tax   _____
Plus postage and handling of $3.00 each   _____
Please gift-wrap at $2.50 each   _____
Total   _____

Make check payable to WMA – *Art in the Kitchen*

Charge to my ____VISA ____MasterCard

Account # _____ Exp. _____

Name_____

Address _____

City _____ State_____ Zip Code _____

____ Please send information on other Museum publications.

____ Please send information on becoming a Friend of the Museum.

Art in the Kitchen
Westmoreland Museum of Art
221 North Main Street
Greensburg, Pennsylvania 15601
Phone: (412) 837-1500   Fax: (412) 837-2921

Please send _____ copies of *Art in the Kitchen* @ 17.95 each   _____
Pennsylvania residents add 6% sales tax   _____
Plus postage and handling of $3.00 each   _____
Please gift-wrap at $2.50 each   _____
Total   _____

Make check payable to WMA – *Art in the Kitchen*

Charge to my ____VISA ____MasterCard

Account # _____ Exp. _____

Name_____

Address _____

City _____ State_____ Zip Code _____

____ Please send information on other Museum publications.

____ Please send information on becoming a Friend of the Museum.

ORDER INFORMATION

Gift-wrap and send to:

Name _____

Address_____

City_____ State ____ Zip Code_____

Gift Card to read:_____

_____

Gift-wrap and send to:

Name _____

Address_____

City_____ State ____ Zip Code_____

Gift Card to read:_____

_____

Gift-wrap and send to:

Name _____

Address_____

City_____ State ____ Zip Code_____

Gift Card to read:_____

_____

Gift-wrap and send to:

Name _____

Address_____

City_____ State ____ Zip Code_____

Gift Card to read:_____

_____